WOMEN, CRIME, AND CHARACTER

WOMEN, CRIME, AND CHARACTER

From Moll Flanders to Tess of the D'Urbervilles

Nicola Lacey

OXFORD
UNIVERSITY PRESS

OXFORD
UNIVERSITY PRESS

Great Clarendon Street, Oxford OX2 6DP

Oxford University Press is a department of the University of Oxford.
It furthers the University's objective of excellence in research, scholarship,
and education by publishing worldwide in

Oxford New York

Auckland Cape Town Dar es Salaam Hong Kong Karachi
Kuala Lumpur Madrid Melbourne Mexico City Nairobi
New Delhi Shanghai Taipei Toronto

With offices in

Argentina Austria Brazil Chile Czech Republic France Greece
Guatemala Hungary Italy Japan Poland Portugal Singapore
South Korea Switzerland Thailand Turkey Ukraine Vietnam

Oxford is a registered trade mark of Oxford University Press
in the UK and in certain other countries

Published in the United States
by Oxford University Press Inc., New York

British Library Cataloguing in Publication Data

Data available

Library of Congress Cataloging in Publication Data

Data available

Typeset by Newgen Imaging Systems (P) Ltd., Chennai, India
Printed in Great Britain
on acid-free paper by
Biddles Ltd., King's Lynn, Norfolk

ISBN 978-0-19-954436-3

10 9 8 7 6 5 4 3 2 1

For my mother, Gill McAndrew
with thanks for the priceless gift of a love of reading

Contents

Foreword

It is a great pleasure and privilege for me to introduce this book, which originates in Professor Nicola Lacey's 2007 Clarendon Law Lectures; 'From Moll Flanders to Tess of the d'Urbervilles'. Professor Lacey is a well-known and influential feminist legal theorist. Her work for, and about, women, is central to her professional life. She was a member of the Prison Reform Trust's Committee of Inquiry into Women's Imprisonment, whose report, *Justice for Women: The Case for Reform*, was published in 2000. As in her book of essays *Unspeakable Subjects* of 1998, she has written widely on feminist legal theory and the rights of women, looking at the ways in which the structure or method of modern law is gendered.

She has published extensively on criminal law, but the book which has attracted wide attention and admiration both within and beyond her own field is her biography of the legal philosopher Herbert Hart, published in 2004 to enviable reviews, and winner of the Swiney Prize for an outstanding book on jurisprudence. The admirable mixture of lucidity, objectivity and sympathy with which this book is written is all the more remarkable given Professor Lacey's close links to her subject—not always an easy position for a biographer. Herbert Hart was a powerful presence at Oxford, and, for a long time, at New College. As a graduate student, and later as a Law Fellow at New College, Professor Lacey came to know him and his family well, and worked closely with his widow Jenifer Hart during the writing of her biography. His thinking had a strong influence on her, particularly in her early publications on the moral justification of punishment. She writes with eloquent clarity about Hart's private struggles, his intellectual history and its context, and what she terms his 'principled liberal social policy', in which, as she puts it, a special significance is accorded 'to individual agency' and to 'the principle of responsibility', notably in the books which she describes so cogently, *Punishment and Responsibility* and *Law, Liberty and Morality*.

It is clear to see the path which links Professor Lacey's work on Hart with her interest in using the realist English novel as a tool for looking at the history of criminal law, as she does in this book, in a move which richly enlarges the developing field of law and literature studies. Hart himself was passionate about great novelists such as Jane Austen, Dickens and Henry James, and you will see that Professor Lacey's own interest in Defoe and Hardy does not take the form of dryasdust legal analysis, but of practical, sensible, sensitive—and illuminating—historical involvement. And, although her work has taken a very different direction from Hart's, she is concerned in this book with individual responsibility and emerging concepts of selfhood.

One of her themes is character evidence. The character evidence for Professor Lacey I propose to put before you is drawn from reviews of her biography: lucid, brilliant, fascinating; sensibility, wit and authority. Her departure point is Moll Flanders, and given the life-style and criminal record of Defoe's heroine, it is perhaps a bit risky to make any character-comparisons there. But I can't resist ending my introduction with Virginia Woolf's account of Moll: 'She has to depend entirely upon her own wits and judgement…Like all Defoe's women, she is a person of robust understanding…Heartless she is not, nor can anyone charge her with levity; but life delights her, and a heroine who lives has us all in tow.'

Hermione Lee
Goldsmiths' Professor of English Literature,
University of Oxford

Preface and acknowledgements

In the early 18th Century, Daniel Defoe found it natural to write a novel whose heroine was a sexually adventurous, socially marginal property offender. Only half a century later, this would have been next to unthinkable. In this book, the disappearance of Moll Flanders, and her supercession in the annals of literary female offenders in the realist tradition by heroines like Tess of the d'Urbervilles, serves as a metaphor for fundamental changes in ideas of selfhood, gender and social order in 18th and 19th Century England. Drawing on law, literature, philosophy and social and economic history, I argue that these broad changes underpinned a radical shift in mechanisms of responsibility-attribution, with decisive implications for the criminalisation of women.

This book is an expanded version of the Clarendon Lectures 2007, which in turn grew out of a broader project which could be described as a socio-legal history of criminal responsibility. This project shares the ambition elegantly expressed in John Baker's Clarendon Lectures seven years ago: to illuminate *The Law's Two Bodies* by bringing its doctrinal and conceptual being into dialogue with its other, harder to reveal, institutional and practical reality. My aim in this work is also to contribute to the small but growing literature which historicises our understanding of key social concepts such as agency, identity, selfhood, responsibility, rights, truth and credibility. So I have aimed to avoid, as Baker put it, 'reading the past backwards', by exploring the meaning of these concepts for contemporaries through a wide range of complementary sources and practices, and by illuminating their fundamental dependence on institutions which develop unevenly across the various interlocking spheres of social space.

I focus in particular on the question of how the treatment and understanding of female criminality was changing during the era which saw the construction of the main building blocks of the modern criminal process, and of how these understandings related in turn to broader ideas about sexual difference, social order and individual agency. The sort of relationship which I attempt to trace is illustrated by the case of Sarah Fletcher, who died in 1799 in Oxfordshire. She must have been a woman of consequence, because she is buried in Dorchester Abbey, where her tombstone records that she died at the age of 29, 'a martyr to excessive sensibility'. The same year, five women (and more than five times as many men) died, by contrast, victims of—if not martyrs to—excessive criminal justice: a small proportion of those actually condemned to death, and a yet smaller one of those whose lives were shortened or otherwise blighted by the direct and indirect effects of the 'Bloody Code'.

This book tells the story of the shifting relationship between informal codes of norms such as the 'culture of sensibility' and the formal system of criminal justice, and of the impact on women and on understandings of femininity of these complementary systems of discipline. It is not, of course, the only story which could be, or has been, told. But I hope that this account, which draws on a wide variety of sources, casts light into corners which remain obscure in accounts informed by a single discipline.

As will be evident from the most cursory reading of this book, I have benefited fundamentally from the painstaking scholarship of historians of criminal justice, from the perceptive readings and contextualisation of historically minded literary critics, and from the imaginative deployment of broad cultural resources in the interpretation of 18th and 19th Century criminal justice by some historians and 'law and literature' scholars. As an amateur in at least (!) three of the four disciplines which animate these lectures, I also count myself especially fortunate to have had overwhelmingly generous advice and encouragement from a large number of friends and colleagues both within and beyond the academy. Since I am both a voracious reader of novels and a serial offender in the business of breaching disciplinary boundaries, it is perhaps perverse that I resisted the genre of law and literature for so long. This resistance began to melt as a result of marvellous conversations with Franco Moretti at the Wissenschaftskolleg in Berlin in 1999–2000, which gradually resolved my uncertainty about how literature could relate to studies not only in the humanities but also in the social sciences. My curiosity received a large boost from the delightful experience of co-organising a workshop in 2003 on George Eliot's *Middlemarch*—the ideal medium for exploring the relationship between literature and the social sciences—with Geoffrey Brennan, Victoria McGeer and David Soskice. Since then, conversations with them, and with Moira Gatens—who generously allowed me to draw on our joint presentation at the *Middlemarch* workshop in these lectures—have stimulated my interest in this most fascinating interdisciplinary world.

During a blissfully peaceful semester at Harvard's Center for European Studies in 2007, I ran up a large debt of gratitude to a number of people who made time for discussions at a crucial point in the development of this project, giving me precious advice and encouragement: Duncan Bell, Janet Halley, Duncan Kennedy, Victoria McGeer, Philip Pettit, Amelie Rorty, Fred Schauer, Carol Steiker, Rosemary Taylor, David Soskice and, particularly, Peter A. Hall, who both made my visit possible and pointed me towards some important sources. Simon Stern was generous in assisting my first tentative steps into 18th Century literary studies, and provided not only advice about reading but also astute comments on an early draft of the lecture from which this book developed. Donna Andrew and John Beattie pointed me towards important historical questions and sources; Malcolm Feeley shared his developing ideas on the debate about the 'vanishing female', and pointed me in the direction of some useful reading. Neil Duxbury, Moira Gatens, Anne Phillips, Jan-Melissa Schramm and Marianna Valverde read and gave exceptionally helpful and generous advice on a draft. My warm thanks go to all of them. For debates about 18th and 19th Century novels and about the history of ideas, and for assistance of various, but always material, kinds, I would also like to express my gratitude to Sally Alexander, Brian Aldiss, Lizzie Barmes, Bianca Beccali, Julia Black, Caroline Forell, Bishnupriya Gupta, Lennie Hoffmann, Jeremy Horder, Frank Kermode, Peter King, Arlie Loughnan, Lee Jackson, Mary Jacobus, Elizabeth Judge, Hermione Lee, Gill McAndrew, Paul McQuail, Ngaire Naffine, Alan Norrie, Finola O'Sullivan, Ursula Owen, James Penner, Alison Soskice, Megan Vaughan and the audience at the University of Toronto's annual Wright lecture in March 2007.

I am, of course, deeply grateful to the Faculty of Law at Oxford University for doing me the honour of inviting me to give the

Clarendon Lectures. Hermione Lee and Lennie Hoffmann distinguished the occasion by chairing the lectures: I am indebted to both of them not only for the exceptionally generous way in which they did so, but also for invaluable discussion of the content of the lectures. My thanks also go to Lucia Zedner, for chairing the seminar following the lectures and, along with Andrew Ashworth, John Gardner, Moira Gatens, Henry Mares and Peter Ramsay, for making it such an intellectually stimulating occasion.

Without the generous support of a Leverhulme Trust Major Research Fellowship, I could not have ventured into the multi-disciplinary terrain which underpins this book: nor would researching and writing it have been such an intellectual pleasure. I am more grateful than I can say for this special privilege.

As ever, my editors at Oxford University Press, Gwen Booth and John Louth, ably assisted by Ros Wallington, have been a tremendous support. I would like them, as well as the three anonymous readers of the manuscript for OUP, to know how warmed I have been by their enthusiasm for this project, and how much I have benefited from their advice.

My special thanks, as always, go to David Soskice, whose unerring enthusiasm and acumen in the search for a convincing argument is an inspiration, and whose enduring faith in my credibility as a transgressor of disciplinary boundaries has been a constant support in the preparation of this book.

Nicola Lacey
London School of Economics,
February 2008

A note on the text

In extracts from legal cases and early novels, some spellings and instances of capitalisation and punctuation may look odd to the reader, conventions of English spelling and punctuation having remained unsettled for most of the 18th Century.

The book includes a large number of notes giving both references and elaborations of particular arguments. The text has been written, however, to stand independently of the notes, which are designed for specialist readers and for those wishing to follow up specific points.

A full citation is given on the first occasion on which each source is referred to, as well as in the Bibliography.

CHAPTER I

'Don't go to murder my character': criminal responsibility in the age of Moll Flanders

In 1722, Daniel Defoe sent out into the world one of the most remarkable female figures in English literature: *Moll Flanders*.[1] Bold, beautiful and brilliantly resourceful, Moll was in many ways ideally qualified for her position as the heroine of one of the first novels in English. She did, however, exhibit one characteristic which we might have expected to exclude her from that position. For most of the novel, her primary occupation consists in a series of distinctly unromantic property offences, including a variety of forms of shoplifting, swindling and even stealing from small children. Born in Newgate gaol of a mother who has escaped execution by 'pleading her belly', and who is transported to Virginia after Moll's birth, Moll escapes her origins at the heart of the criminal underworld in her early life, only to be forced to return to it after the death of her first husband, when want of wealth and birth prevent her from finding a secure position in respectable society. Using her beauty, ingenuity and cunning, Moll escapes poverty and makes her way through late 17th Century England by means of property crime, before ultimately being caught, convicted and transported to Virginia along with one of her five husbands, himself a convicted highwayman. Adding colour to this pattern of thieving and deception, Moll enjoys an active and varied love life,

---

[1] Daniel Defoe, *Moll Flanders* (1722: Penguin Classics 1989).

encompassing both incest and bigamy, with plentiful instances of the more quotidian diversions of fornication and adultery thrown in for good measure.

Ostensibly, Moll Flanders is a tale of sin and repentance. While awaiting her punishment in Newgate, Moll experiences a mental collapse and renounces her criminal habits. She is ultimately rewarded with riches and success gained by good fortune and legitimate use of her prodigious talents. It is nonetheless hard for the modern reader entirely to believe in her reformation. For the new, respectable, wealthy Moll is the very same Moll as the thieving and deceiving Moll, and for a morality tale, the painful moments of her regret and punishment are extraordinarily brief. As Juliet Mitchell aptly put it, Moll is 'a small-time capitalist in the making, she is the pilgrim progressing to what, as a sharp-witted child and clear-headed woman, she rightly takes to be the capitalist definition of a gentlewoman—the wife of a prosperous businessman or a self-made woman in her own right...it is not the righteous ending that prevents Moll from being a porno-graphic tale of wickedness but rather the fact that Moll is good even while a thief and a prostitute and just as bad or just as good even while she is a wife and investor.'[2] It is as if—in stark contrast, for example, to John Bunyan's Christian in The Pilgrim's Progress (1678)—Defoe's genius in creating Moll's vividly autonomous personality outstrips his moral purpose. If Defoe's message was that redemption is always available to the true penitent, it must also be said that he conveys very forcefully that wit, courage and enterprise are valuable attributes for a woman; and it is these which ultimately make of Moll a successful gentlewoman as much as a successful thief.

Before turning to Moll's literary cousin, Tess of the d'Urbervilles, it is worth pausing to note the striking contrast between Defoe's image of female criminality and that to be found in criminology—a discipline which of course belongs firmly to the age of Tess. Women's relatively low representation among offenders, and the strong association of notions of criminality and deviance with characteristics culturally marked as masculine, consigned female

[2] Juliet Mitchell, 'Moll Flanders, The Rise of Capitalist Woman' pp. 195–218 of Women: The Longest Revolution (London: Virago 1984) pp. 203–4; reprinted from her introduction to the Penguin edition of Moll Flanders (Harmondsworth 1978).

offenders to the outer margins of the discipline until the pioneering work of feminist writers like Carol Smart in the 1970s.[3] As feminist criminologists noted, women offenders tend to be thought of as weak-minded or mad rather than bad: or, when engaged in behaviour sufficiently subversive of conventional norms of femininity, as 'doubly deviant'. Female offenders also tend to be seen as victims: victims of their hormones, of their circumstances and, sometimes, of men. The idea that choices, agency or reason are important factors in their offending behaviour surfaces implicitly in theories rooted in distinctively gendered opportunity structures, but is rarely emphasised (and here feminist criminologists have sometimes unwittingly echoed the assumptions of the criminological traditions which they criticise).[4] The female gendering of particular defences such as mental incapacity defences like diminished responsibility (as opposed to 'masculine' defences like provocation and self-defence) has also been widely noted.[5] The criminological image of the female offender has often approached the ultimate stereotype of conventional femininity: passive rather than active; driven by emotion rather than reason; moved by impulses located in the body rather than the mind.

Moll Flanders could not stand in greater contrast to this stereotyped image. For Moll is a thoroughly autonomous woman, brimming with agency and enterprise: she has plans and ambitions; she has strategies for pursuing them; she reflects upon, and has an account of, her own behaviour[6]—explicitly linking the need to steal with her insecure position in society and lack of legitimate means of support, and on occasion inveighing against the sexual double standard. Though hardly burdened with an overactive superego,

[3] Carol Smart, *Women, Crime and Criminology* (London: Sage 1976); see also Ngaire Naffine, *Female Crime: the construction of women in criminology* (Sydney: Allen and Unwin 1987); Frances Heidensohn, *Women and Crime* (New York University Press 1985); Allison Morris, *Women, Crime and Criminal Justice* (Oxford: Basil Blackwell 1987).

[4] As Garthine Walker has argued, the same has often been true of historical accounts: *Crime, Gender and Social Order in Early Modern England* (Cambridge University Press 2003) Chapter 6. Walker's book by contrast gives a central place to women's agency.

[5] For example by Susan Edwards, *Women on Trial* (Manchester University Press 1984).

[6] In precisely the style of Charles Taylor's self-interpreting human subject: *Sources of the Self: The Making of Modern Identity* (Cambridge University Press 1989).

she has a conscience, and feels shame and guilt about both her unwittingly incestuous marriage and her momentary temptation to kill. She also suffers feelings and perplexities which we would be inclined to associate with the experience of a much later version of capitalism: even when she has become wealthy through crime, she finds that she is unable to give up the thrill of stealing and, in a manner somewhere between conspicuous consumption and addiction to risk, continues until she is caught. Perhaps most significantly, Moll is a strong, active and dominant woman, and her world is peopled by several other women similar to herself (notably her 'governess', a high-class receiver and pawnbroker). The men in this world are, by contrast, often weak, indecisive and passive. Some critics have suggested that Moll is in effect gendered masculine:[7] Virginia Woolf noted that she was a 'person rather than a woman',[8] and one recent biographer has even gone so far as to suggest that she represented Defoe's alter ego—an outlet for some of the more exotic predispositions of her gloriously complicated, bisexual creator.[9] Whatever the truth of these assertions, the key point for our purposes is that Moll's literary success implies that her early readers received her as entirely plausible. Moll Flanders is, in short, a fully responsible subject, and the very antithesis of the frail, emotional, dominated woman one might have expected to find in a novel of its time.

Let us now jump forward to the late 19th Century, and to a very different female heroine: *Tess of the D'Urbervilles*, who appeared to sharply divided public reaction in 1891.[10] Moll and Tess share

---

[7] See in particular Ian Watt, *The Rise of the Novel: Studies in Defoe, Richardson and Fielding* (University of California Press 1957) p. 113; Hal Gladfelder, *Criminality and Narrative in Eighteenth Century England* (London and Baltimore: Johns Hopkins University Press 2001) Chapter 7.

[8] *The Common Reader* (1925: New York: Harvest, Harcourt 1984) pp. 86–94.

[9] See, variously, Juliet Mitchell, 'Moll Flanders, The Rise of Capitalist Woman', op. cit.; John Martin, *Beyond Belief: The Real Life of Daniel Defoe* (Ebbw Vale: Accent Press 2006). Martin's speculation is not out of line with the more judicious analysis offered by Watt, who noted that Moll was 'suspiciously like her author' (*The Rise of the Novel* op. cit. p. 113).

[10] First published 1891: Bantam Classic 2004. Though *Tess* met with critical acclaim, many of her early readers were scandalised by the book, not least by Hardy's treatment of sex. In fact Hardy had modified the manuscript between its serialisation in the *Illustrated London News* and its publication in book form in order to soften the implication of Tess's active collusion in her relationship with Alec D'Urberville, so sharply hostile was initial reaction to the original implication of her active sexual agency. I am grateful to Mary Jacobus for alerting me to

certain characteristics: both are beautiful, both are proud of their beauty and have a sense of themselves as special, an aspiration to transcend their difficult origins;[11] both have significant resources of determination; both feel lasting emotional attachments; and both commit offences. But here the resemblance ends. Notwithstanding her relatively respectable origins, Tess's tale is one of a human being destroyed by her circumstances and, ultimately, by her own decisions. Her crime—which, significantly, takes place behind doors which the reader is not allowed to open—is a crime of passion: the murder of the man who, by raping her, set in motion the train of events which leads to her ruin. And her punishment is swift, decisive and annihilating—despite the fact that, unlike Moll, she is certainly not represented as a danger to society. Hardy suggests a number of causes for Tess's ultimate act of revenge, several of which evoke late Victorian images of female criminal pathology: a hereditary capacity for impulsive acts of violence and a dissociation of the will from the body notable among them.[12] Yet Tess is not—as one might have expected from a late 19th Century novel treating female crime—an image of female weak-mindedness or incapacity. What Hardy most certainly gives us in Tess, however, is an image of female powerlessness; of the futility of female self-assertion or rebellion; and of the punishment of sexual non-conformity. Like most female offenders who feature, as heroines or otherwise, in 19th Century novels—they are mainly husband-murderers, infanticides and prostitutes—Tess's position as a woman underlines her social powerlessness: notwithstanding her strong sense of personal responsibility, and her creator's evident indictment of the sexual double standard, this late Victorian heroine, unlike Moll, is not able—or, rather, not allowed—to shape her own destiny. While Defoe allows Moll to assert her strong sense of self—at one point, cutting off a digression about her husband, she insists, 'this is my story, not his'...[13]—Tess's self-assertion leads to disaster.

this point: for further analysis, see her 'Tess's Purity', 26 *Essays in Criticism* (1976) 318–38, reprinted as 'Tess: The Making of a Pure Woman', in Susan Lipshitz (ed.), *Tearing the Veil: Essays on Femininity* (London: Routledge and Kegan Paul 1978) pp. 77–92. See further the discussion of Hardy's prefaces to later editions in Chapter III.

[11] Tess 'knew herself to be more impassioned in nature, cleverer, more beautiful' than her fellow milkmaids: *Tess of the d'Urbervilles* op. cit. p. 151.

[12] *Tess of the d'Urbervilles* op. cit. pp. 401, 406, 394–5.

[13] *Moll Flanders* op. cit. p. 380; cf. *Roxana or, The Fortunate Mistress* (1724: Oxford World's Classics 1996), Defoe's other—and equally vivid—female protagonist.

In this book, I will argue that this change has to do not so much with the disappearance of feminine agency: rather, it is a question of the social consequences of women's exercise of their agency and self-expression, which are themselves consequences of shifting vectors of identity, gender and social order in modernising England. By the time of Tess, the idea of a figure such as Moll Flanders—a sassy, cunning, warm and rather successful property offender and manipulator of men—as the unambiguous *heroine* of a novel would be unthinkable. The closest 19th Century literary analogy to Moll—Becky Sharp, anti-heroine of Thackeray's *Vanity Fair* (1847–8),[14] and someone whom we shall be meeting again—is decisively punished for the unscrupulous use to which she puts her intellect and resourcefulness. Devoid of Moll's humane qualities, Becky is not so much a heroine as the device which Thackeray uses to hold up to ridicule the corruption of Regency society. And though he is undoubtedly the creator of Victorian fiction's most spectacularly intelligent female figure, in Becky's friend Amelia, Thackeray also gives voice to the emerging stereotype of female weakness: of her son, he comments that 'He had been brought up by a kind, weak, and tender woman, who had no pride about anything but about him, and whose heart was so pure and whose bearing was so meek and humble that she could not but needs be a true lady. She busied herself in gentle offices and quiet duties; if

Like Moll's, Roxana's is a tale of sin and repentance, but Roxana even goes so far as to meditate on whether her repentance was caused by conscience or by misery: after all, she reflects, she did not repent when still fortunate...Defoe's work has sometimes been marginalised in accounts of the development of the novel, not least because of his concern with 'impolite' spheres of life relegated to the margins of the 18th Century novel from Richardson on, and the close association of *Moll* and *Roxana* with the genres of gallows speeches and rogue autobiography to which Defoe was also a contributor: see J. Paul Hunter, *Before Novels: the cultural contexts of eighteenth-century English fiction* (New York: Norton 1990). For the definitive defence of Defoe as one important founder of the realist novel, see Watt, *The Rise of the Novel* op. cit. Chapters III and IV; and Michael McKeon, *The Origins of the English Novel 1600–1740* (Johns Hopkins University Press 1987) Chapter 9. Gladfelder, too, has argued persuasively for Defoe's place in the tradition, pointing out that his genre of gritty realism anticipates in some ways the much later work of Balzac and Stendhal: *Criminality and Narrative in Eighteenth Century England* op. cit. pp. 5ff.

[14] (1848: Revised edition 1851: Penguin Classics 2001). Significantly for my argument, the subtitle is 'A Novel without a Hero'. Cf. Lydia Gwilt, anti-heroine of Wilkie Collins' *Armadale* (1866: Penguin Classics 1995): for a discussion of the salience of deviant women in such 'sensation novels', and their ambiguous place in the realist tradition, see Chapter III.

she never said brilliant things, she never spoke or thought unkind ones; guileless and artless, loving and pure, indeed how could our poor little Amelia be other than a real gentlewoman!'[15]

In making this argument about the changing terrain over which it was regarded as appropriate for women to act, I also want to explore what the 19th Century unthinkability of Moll Flanders signifies about both the images of women's autonomy and the reality of women's criminality in the flow of historical development through the 18th and 19th Centuries. This was, of course, the period in which the institutional cornerstones of the modern, adversarial criminal trial were gradually being put in place. Those of us interested in this complex process of 'modernisation' are fortunate to be able to draw on a rich historiography illuminating the highly discretionary and decentralised nature of 18th Century criminal justice from which it proceeded.[16] Criminal justice was largely administered at the local level: assize judges travelling the circuits from London carried the personal authority of the monarch, but it was rather the authority of local landowners and, later, clerics, relatively well-to-do merchants and industrialists in their capacity as Justices which shaped the application of the law. This was a system which, particularly from the mid-18th Century on, certainly merited its nickname, 'the Bloody Code': the 50 capital statutes on the books at the time of the Restoration in 1660 had risen, by the early 19th Century, to over 200. With no organised police force, let alone prosecuting authority, the (inevitably uneven) enforcement of criminal law depended on private initiative—a system which, as Henry Fielding was quick to point out both in his political and reformist writing and in his novels,[17] was wide open to corruption. The attitudes and assumptions of those prosecuting crime, those testifying as witnesses, those acting as filters on

[15] Ibid, p. 654.
[16] In what follows, I am drawing in particular on John M. Beattie, *Crime and the Courts in England 1660–1800* (Princeton University Press 1986) and 'Scales of Justice' 9 *Law and History Review* (1991) 221; Peter King, *Crime, Justice and Discretion 1740–1820* (Oxford University Press 2000) and *Crime and Law in England 1750–1840* (Past and Present Publications: Cambridge University Press 2006); Douglas Hay, 'Property, Authority and Criminal Law' in D. Hay, P. Linebaugh and E.P. Thompson (eds.), *Albion's Fatal Tree* (Harmondsworth, Penguin 1975), pp. 17–63; John H. Langbein, *The Origins of Adversary Criminal Trial* (Oxford University Press 2003).
[17] See in particular *Jonathan Wild* (1743: Oxford World's Classics 2003).

grand juries, not to mention of petty trial juries and Justices at the
Quarter Sessions which heard the vast bulk of criminal cases, were
therefore crucial in shaping the operation of the process.[18] And
though the 18th Century saw—to use John Langbein's term[19]—the
gradual 'lawyerisation' of the trial, this development applied primarily to assize cases. (Though numbers are a crude measure of
their relative importance, it is perhaps worth noting here that it has
been estimated that there were about 5,000 Justices, as opposed to
just 12 Assize Judges, in 18th Century England.[20]) Notwithstanding
the recognition, particularly in London, of the disadvantages of
this discretionary and dis-organised 'system' as early as the late
17th Century,[21] the dynamics of criminalisation were shaped to a
yet greater extent than today by non-official actors right through
to the 19th Century. In trying to reconstruct how their decisions
were made, and the broader context in which criminalisation took
place, literary resources are a crucial complement to contemporary
pamphlets, case reports and court records.[22]

[18] On the extensive power of Justices at this period, see Norma Landau, *The
Justices of the Peace 1679–1760* (Berkeley and Los Angeles: University of California
Press 1984).
[19] John H. Langbein, *The Origins of Adversary Criminal Trial* op. cit.
[20] See Bruce Lenman and Geoffrey Parker, 'The State, the Community and
Criminal Law in Early Modern Europe', in V.A.C. Gatrell, Bruce Lenman and
Geoffrey Parker (eds.), *Crime and the Law* (Europa 1980) p. 11 at p. 32; see also
Peter King, *Crime and Law in England* op. cit. pp. 47–50; Norma Landau, *The
Justice of the Peace 1679–1760* op. cit.
[21] J.M. Beattie, *Crime and the Courts in England* op. cit. pp. 621–4; John
Langbein, *The Origins of Adversary Criminal Trial* op. cit. Chapter 3.
[22] As recent work by scholars like Dana Rabin, Martin Wiener, Jan-Melissa
Schramm and Lisa Rodensky has amply shown; see Martin Wiener, *Reconstructing
the Criminal* (Cambridge University Press 1991); Dana Y. Rabin, *Identity, Crime, and
Legal Responsibility in Eighteenth-Century England* (Palgrave Macmillan 2004); Jan-
Melissa Schramm, *Testimony and Advocacy in Victorian Law, Literature and Theology*
(Cambridge University Press 2000); Lisa Rodensky, *The Crime in Mind: Criminal
Responsibility and the Victorian Novel* (Oxford University Press 2003); see also Philip
Collins, *Dickens and Crime* (2nd ed, London: Macmillan 1965); Peter Brooks,
The Melodramatic Imagination (Columbia University Press 1985) and *Troubling
Confessions: Speaking Guilt in Law and Literature* (Chicago University Press 2000);
John Bender, *Imagining the Penitentiary: Fiction and the Architecture of Mind in
Eighteenth Century England* (University of Chicago Press 1987). The field of 'law
and literature' scholarship is both vast and diverse. For classic texts, see Richard
H. Weisberg and Jean-Pierre Barricelli, 'Literature and the Law', in Joseph
Gibaldi and Barricelli (eds.), *Interrelations of Literature* (New York: MLA 1982);
James Boyd White, *Acts of Hope: Creating Authority in Literature, Law and Politics*
(University of Chicago Press 1995). For helpful analysis of the various genres
of 'law and literature' scholarship, see Ian Ward, *Law and Literature: Possibilities*

Beyond the mystery of Moll's demise amid the modernising process, a further reason for examining specifically the development of attitudes to women's agency and responsibility lies in an intriguing debate between historians of crime and punishment about levels of female criminality. In the turbulent history of criminal justice, most criminologists would agree that one of the few constants, across widely divergent societies, is the relatively low representation of women among those accused and convicted of crime.[23] In contemporary England and Wales, for example, women make up about a fifth of known offenders.[24] Though the assessment of crime figures before the inception of public statistics in the early 19th Century is a notoriously tricky matter, the gradual accretion of historical research on local records now allows for some estimates. These suggest that, in England, women made up a relatively small minority of offenders officially proceeded against from at least the 14th Century on.[25] The degree to which the recorded difference reflects specificities of women's behaviour as opposed to different responses to female and male conduct has, of course, been debated. And, reflecting the different poles of this debate, the official 'underrepresentation' of women has in turn been 'explained' in terms of, on the one hand, assertions of female passivity, weakness, incapacity, lack of opportunity, strong socialisation to conformity or powerlessness, and, on the other, claims about leniency or 'chivalry' towards women.[26]

and Perspectives (Cambridge University Press 1995); Maria Aristodemou, Law and Literature: Journeys from Her to Eternity (Oxford University Press 2000); and Kieran Dolin, A Critical Introduction to Law and Literature (Cambridge University Press 2007), Chapter 4 of which pays particular attention to the interplay between legal and literary sources in the development of 18th Century criminal justice—an interplay the strength of which was, Dolin argues, somewhat diluted by the gradual formalisation and professionalisation of law from the late 18th Century on.

[23] Doreen Elliot, Gender, Delinquency and Society (Aldershot: Avebury 1988) Chapter 1; Allison Morris, Women, Crime and Criminal Justice op. cit. pp. 18–19
[24] Frances Heidensohn and Loraine Gelsthorpe, 'Gender and Crime', in Mike Maguire, Rod Morgan and Robert Reiner (eds.), The Oxford Handbook of Criminology (4th ed, Oxford University Press 2007) p. 381, at p. 391.
[25] Jenny Kermode and Garthine Walker (eds.), Women, Crime and the Courts in Early Modern England (UCL Press 1994), Introduction p. 4. As Kermode and Walker note, however, the broader significance of these estimates must be assessed with caution, not least because of the male orientation of offence categories.
[26] For an overview of these theories, see Smart, Women, Crime and Criminology op. cit.; in relation to the 18th and 19th Centuries, see, respectively, Peter King, Crime and Law in England op. cit. Chapters 5 and 6 and Martin Wiener, Men

In 1981, however, Malcolm Feeley and Deborah Little published what has become an influential paper on 'The Vanishing Female: the decline of women in the criminal process 1687–1912'.[27] The paper presented figures from the Old Bailey (London's principal criminal court) which suggested that the proportion of women charged with felonies dropped from, on average, a hefty 40% in 1680 to a mere 10% by the end of the 19th Century. In the first decade of the 18th Century, women even outnumbered men as defendants at the Old Bailey.[28] Feeley and Little charted a relatively steady decline from the early 18th Century, albeit punctuated by spikes related to specific social conditions such as war or economic disruption.[29] Similarly high levels of female crime in the late 17th and early 18th Centuries have been reported by other historians working on Cheshire and on the North East of England,[30] while John Beattie's Surrey data[31] also confirm a higher (though less striking) proportion of female property offenders in the areas nearest to London. On the basis of this evidence, the plausibility of Moll Flanders in the early 18th Century, succeeded by her literary unthinkability by its close, would seem to map on to a real decline in the recorded criminality of women.

of Blood: Violence, Manliness and Criminal Justice in Victorian England (Cambridge University Press 2004) Chapter 4.

[27] 25 Law and Society Review (1981) 719; see also Malcolm Feeley, 'The Decline of Women in the Criminal Process: A Comparative History' 15 Criminal Justice History (1994) 235–74.

[28] By contrast, women made up only an eighth of prosecutors and victims at the Old Bailey between 1674 and 1834—a fact which may speak to the difficult economic situation of women, and of single women in particular, in London: see further Chapters II and III below.

[29] See also David F. Greenberg, 'The Gendering of Crime in Marxist Theory', in Greenberg (ed.), Crime and Capitalism: Readings in Marxist Criminology (2nd ed, Temple University Press 1993); Greenberg's further analysis of the Old Bailey records confirms the trajectory identified by Feeley and Little.

[30] See, respectively, Garthine Walker, 'Women, Theft and the World of Stolen Goods' in Kermode and Walker Women, Crime and the Courts in Early Modern England op. cit. (women as 38% of theft defendants in 1660s Cheshire); Walker, Crime, Gender and Social Order in Early Modern England op. cit. Chapter 5; Gwenda Morgan and Peter Rushton, Rogues, Thieves and the Rule of Law: the problem of law enforcement in north-east England, 1718–1800 (London: UCL Press 1998) Chapter 3 (women over 50% of those charged with theft in Newcastle, and at least a third over the whole North East region).

[31] J.M. Beattie, 'The Criminality of Women in Eighteenth Century England' 8 Journal of Social History (1975) 80–116.

More recently, however, Peter King has challenged Feeley and Little's interpretation.[32] Telling a story of continuity, King argues that data from a variety of regions suggest no significant change in the proportion of female offenders between the mid-18th and mid-19th Centuries. Further arguments calling the 'vanishing female' hypothesis into question are that inclusion of data on the less serious cases heard at Quarter Sessions would generate less striking results; that Feeley and Little's overall trajectory is distorted by the fact that their figures begin during what is generally acknowledged to have been an exceptional period; that the frequency of wars during the 18th Century underpins the relatively high averages of known female offending;[33] and that in any case the relatively high proportions of women recorded in the last decades of the 17th Century and the very early 18th Century (abutting, incidentally, the period in which Defoe sets Moll Flanders) were mostly to be found in London and other urban areas.

To come to a decisive view of the rights and wrongs of this debate would be beyond the scope of my project. But I hope to illuminate some of the questions at issue by re-examining it in the light of both literary sources and historical data about women's changing social position. The strikingly high proportion of women prosecuted at the Old Bailey in the late 17th and early 18th Centuries must have some significance; and the juxtaposition of this focus on women's criminality with the appearance of Moll Flanders is telling. What do the attitudes to women represented in literature—attitudes to their autonomy, capacity for responsible agency, and social role—suggest about their likely treatment in the criminal process, and how do these match up with what we know about women's position in contemporary economy and society?

---

[32] See Peter King, *Crime and Law in England* op. cit. Chapter 6 and, advancing a more general argument about the relatively lenient treatment of women over the period of his study, including an estimate that men were 25% less likely than women to be acquitted, Chapter 5; see also King, *Crime Justice and Discretion* op. cit. pp. 196–207; J. M. Beattie, *Policing and Punishment in London 1660–1750: Urban Crime and the Limits of Terror* (Oxford University Press 2001) pp. 20, 56, 63–72, 335–7, 356.

[33] King, op. cit. p. 213.

Conduct, Character and Responsibility in 18th Century Criminal Justice

In what follows, I will draw on a set of hypotheses about the broad development of ideas of responsibility for crime which I have mapped out and defended in greater detail elsewhere, and for which I will offer only a sketchy justification here.[34] My starting assumption is that specific patterns of responsibility-attribution relate to various roles and needs of a criminal justice system: a need for legitimation, and a practical need to specify and co-ordinate the sorts of knowledge which can be brought into a court room. The imperatives set by these needs for legitimation and co-ordination are, needless to say, changing over time, as the political, cultural, economic and institutional environment of the criminal process shifts. In the early 18th Century, most criminal trials were a highly non-technical affair: a conversation between the accused and the court—trial, as John Langbein has put it, as altercation.[35] Levels of lawyers' involvement—with the important exception of treason trials and certain other highly technical areas such as forgery—were low: felony defendants had no right to be represented by Counsel until 1836, and though judges were increasingly balancing prosecutors' resort to lawyers by exercising their discretion to allow counsel to engage in examination of witnesses from the middle of the 18th Century, they had no right to address the jury until the passage of the Prisoners' Counsel Act in 1836.[36] The average length of a criminal trial in the last decades of the 18th Century has

[34] See in particular Nicola Lacey, 'In Search of the Responsible Subject: History, Philosophy and Criminal Law Theory' 64 *Modern Law Review* (2001) 350–71; 'Responsibility and Modernity in Criminal Law' 9 *Journal of Political Philosophy* (2001) 249–77.

[35] *The Origins of Adversary Criminal Trial* op. cit.; see also Stephan Landsman, 'The Rise of the Contentious Spirit: Adversary Procedure in Eighteenth Century England' 75 *Cornell Law Review* (1990) 497–609.

[36] This particular institutional arrangement itself drew the critical eye of novelists, including George Eliot (see *Felix Holt: The Radical* (1866: Penguin Classics 1995) p. 367); Henry Fielding *The History of Tom Jones, A Foundling* (1749: Oxford World Classics 1996) Book VIII Chapter II; and Walter Scott, *The Heart of Midlothian* (1818: Penguin Classics 1994). Set in the early 18th Century, this last novel includes a detailed picture of the Scottish criminal justice system, and observations on the respects in which it was more humane than that of England, including the provision for legal representation of defendants. On the history of the 1836 legislation and its role in shaping the adversarial criminal trial, see

been estimated at between 20 and 30 minutes, with Assizes hearing between 20 and 30 cases a day. This in turn lends weight to the judgment of one of the most influential historians of the period that the criminal trial operated up to the early 19th Century on something far closer to a presumption of guilt than a presumption of innocence (a doctrine which, like the special criminal standard of proof, in any case received no judicial formulation until the late 18th century).[37]

While treatises and commentaries on criminal law and its doctrines had of course existed for several centuries, their impact on run-of-the-mill cases can all too easily be over-estimated, particularly in the light of the dominance of trial before Justices of the Peace already noted. Here we run into the problem which animated John Baker's fascinating Clarendon Lectures in 2000: 'How can we understand legal history…if the authoritative sources, the case-law found in the reports and the records, even the statutes, do not tell us what the law truly is or was?'[38] While, as Baker acknowledged, this problem is relevant even to contemporary legal scholarship, it is a particular issue in relation to periods and areas of legal practice in which there is reason to think that the law's canonical, doctrinal body was a particularly poor indicator of its living, institutional body. And this is certainly the case in relation to criminal law of the 18th Century. Until well into the 19th Century, there was neither systematic law reporting nor formalised legal education, and there was no regular system of appeals through which points of law could be tested until 1908.[39]

David J.A. Cairns, *Advocacy and the Making of the English Criminal Trial 1800–1865* (Oxford: Clarendon Press 1998).

[37] See further Langbein, ibid, p. 263; 'Shaping the Eighteenth Century Criminal Trial: A View from the Ryder Sources' 50 *University of Chicago Law Review* 1 (1983) 82ff; and 'The Criminal Trial before the Lawyers' 45 *University of Chicago Law Review* (1978) 236; see also Beattie, *Crime and the Courts in England* op. cit. p. 630; and Dana Rabin, *Identity, Crime and Legal Responsibility* op. cit. p. 29. Even in late 19th Century Kent, Conley found the presumption of innocence operating largely in favour of the respectable: Carolyn A. Conley, *The Unwritten Law: Criminal Justice in Victorian Kent* (Oxford University Press 1991) p. 57ff; Bruce Smith: 'The Presumption of Guilt in the English Law of Theft 1750–1850' 23 *Law and History Review* (2005) 23 (with critical response by Norma Landau).

[38] J.H. Baker, *The Law's Two Bodies: Some Evidential Problems in English Legal History* (Oxford: Clarendon Press 2001) p. 1.

[39] On the diffusion of knowledge about legal decisions during this period, and on the limited possibilities for appeal, particularly from Quarter Sessions, see Peter King, *Crime and Law in England* op. cit. Chapter 1, esp. pp. 14ff, 32ff.

The law of criminal evidence, too, was still developing throughout the period, and would not be put together in systematic form until the late 19th Century.[40] As Schramm aptly sums up the position, "an inchoate notion of the standard of proof in criminal cases' led to the expectation that a man would not be convicted unless the evidence of his guilt was plainly manifest, and it was believed that the 'facts' of the case which emerged from the accused's admissions would in some way guarantee the discovery of the truth'.[41]

Happily, a detailed historiography, based not only on law reports and treatises but also on judges' notes and contemporary eyewitness accounts, now gives us some insight into the actual practice of 18th Century criminal law. This suggests that the overwhelming bulk of evidence was either eye-witness testimony or evidence as to the defendant's or complainant's character and reputation. Such evidence was focused on the accused's reputation and social position, but inferences about disposition appear to have been a natural corollary. Since the accused's confrontation with the jury was the kernel of the trial, wherever direct evidence of conduct was ambiguous, the jury's assumptions about his or her character (and that of witnesses) were central to the chances of exculpation: to judgments of credibility, to the reception of pleas for mercy, and to the likelihood of partial verdicts—all crucial matters in a trial

In relation to assize cases, before the creation of the Court for Crown Cases Reserved in the mid-19th Century, difficult cases might be referred to colleagues on a Judge's return to London; but neither this nor the CCR amounted to a systematic appellate process of the sort regarded, from the 20th Century on, as central to a precedent-based system. Private law reporting was, of course, well established, but by its nature concentrated on exceptional cases. On legal education, see K.J.M. Smith, *Lawyers, Legislators and Theorists* (Oxford University Press 1998) Chapter 12; Allyson M. May, *The Bar and the Old Bailey 1750–1850* (University of North Carolina Press 2003); David Cairns *Advocacy and the Making of the English Criminal Trial 1800–1865* op. cit.

[40] T.P. Gallanis, 'The Rise of Modern Evidence Law' 84 *Iowa Law Review* (1999) 499; see also Barbara Shapiro, 'Religion and the Law: evidence, proof and "matter of fact", 1660–1700', in Norma Landau (ed.), *Law Crime and English Society 1660–1830* (Cambridge University Press 2002) p. 185; and Shapiro's *Probability and Certainty in Seventeenth-Century England: A Study of the Relationships between Natural Science, Religion, History, Law and Literature* (Princeton University Press 1983); C.J.W. Allen, *The Law of Evidence in Victorian England* (Cambridge University Press 1997).

[41] *Testimony and Advocacy in Victorian Law, Literature and Theology* op. cit. p. 52: the quotation is drawn from John Langbein, 'The Criminal Trial Before the Lawyers', op. cit. at pp. 307–8. Cf. the confident assertion in *R v Blandy* (1752) 18 *State Trials* 1118 at 1187 that 'facts cannot lie', on which see Schramm p. 58.

often focused on the key question of whether the death penalty would apply or not.[42]

One wonders, for example, how dispassionately the jury was able to assess the credibility of a certain Joseph Howells, otherwise known—as the heading to the report in the Old Bailey Sessions Papers[43] records—as 'Lying Joe'. It seems likely that his conviction for Grand Larceny on October 16th 1745 was more or less assured when one of the witnesses gave the following testimony: 'I went to a publick house to enquire after him, and described him; and there was a man with a black cap and a chew of tobacco in his mouth, and he said he knew him, and that he went by the name of Lying Joe, and was as great a villain as any in England, then I thought I should lose my money.'[44] (The unfortunate Joe was accordingly sentenced to transportation.) Another good example is Dorothy Copping, tried in 1688 for coining, 'as having a File, a pair of Cutting Sheers, and some Clipping found about her. Upon whose Tryal it was evident, That she had often [had] Clipped Monies, and brag'd of the quantities she had put off; and there being furthermore a Shilling new Clipped in her possession, though she alledged she found it, and that her Employ was to carry Loads as a Basket Woman; yet

---

[42] J.M. Beattie, 'Scales of Justice' op. cit. at p. 231–2; see also Dana Rabin, *Identity, Crime and Legal Responsibility* op. cit. p. 18 (an illuminating book, though one which in my view overplays the impact of legal doctrines). As the trial scenes in both *Felix Holt* (op. cit. pp. 440ff) and Elizabeth Gaskell's *Mary Barton* (1859: Penguin Classics 1980) demonstrate, character evidence still loomed large in the first half of 19th Century, but its power was diminishing, just as the inferences which could be drawn from it legally were gradually reduced. On the practice of drawing inferences of conduct from hearsay evidence well into the 19th Century, see T.P. Gallanis, 'The Rise of Modern Evidence Law', op. cit. pp. 499ff. Gallanis argues persuasively that the gradual development of exclusionary rules in the second half of the 18th Century was itself a function of the slow infiltration of defence lawyers: since they were at this stage barred from addressing the jury, it was particularly important for them to mount arguments to prevent prejudicial forms of evidence from reaching the jury in the first place. On the status orientation of character evidence, see Kieran Dolin, *A Critical Introduction to Law and Literature* (Cambridge University Press 2007) p. 113.

[43] These reports, written for a lay audience, are an invaluable resource, though one which requires careful interpretation, not least because of the uneven standard and completeness of the reports over different periods. For further discussion, see Joel Peter Eigen, *Witnessing Insanity: Madness and Mad-Doctors in the English Court* (Yale University Press 1995) pp. 7–8; John H. Langbein, *The Origins of Adversary Criminal Trial* op. cit. pp. 182–190.

[44] Old Bailey Sessions Papers t17451016-7.

upon the Character given of her, the Jury found her Guilty of the Trespass.'[45] Conversely Sarah Hill, indicted for theft of valuable silver in 1696, was able to rely on evidence of good character: 'It appeared upon the Trial that her Husband had left the silver with her, who is since fled. She called abundance of People to her Reputation, who gave a very good Character of her, but said that her Husband was a very ill liver. The Jury taking it into Consideration acquitted her.'[46]

Character evidence was also central to the pre- and post-trial processes, which formed a yet more influential aspect of the practice of criminalisation in the 18th and early 19th Centuries than they do today. As late as 1830, Richard Perrara, convicted of theft, was 'recommended to mercy by the jury on account of his character, and believing him to have been seduced by Griffiths' (his female co-defendant).[47] In filtering cases for trial, individual Justices and Grand Juries would draw on local knowledge of the defendant's reputation, feeding into the assumption that those selected for trial were guilty. And in the elaborate and equally discretionary process of considering pleas for reprieve from the death penalty or pardons,[48] those without credible witnesses able and willing to testify to their character stood little chance of success—a fact which explains the special disabilities under which itinerant workers and migrants to urban areas laboured.[49] On the other side of the coin, the strong reliance of both formal and informal mechanisms of social control on networks of information about reputation helps to explain the persistent elite concern with vagrancy. It also helps to explain why the figures show distinctive patterns of criminalisation in the cities, where networks of communication and reputation were less robust, and hence a less potent resource for the criminal process. In this context, a functional presumption of guilt became a particularly important resource for the system: the defendant who was unable

[45] Old Bailey Sessions Papers t16881205–25, 5 December 1688.
[46] Old Bailey Sessions Papers t16960909–23, 9 September 1696; cf Jane Collins, acquitted on 13 January 1716 t17160113–44.
[47] Old Bailey Sessions Papers t18300415–140: note that the court had no difficulty in ascribing primary agency to his female co-defendant.
[48] See King, *Crime, Justice and Discretion* op. cit. Chapter 9; V.A.C. Gatrell, *The Hanging Tree: Execution and the English People* (Oxford University Press 1994).
[49] On the greater reluctance to show leniency to those not members of the immediate community, see Peter King, *Crime, Justice and Discretion* op. cit. pp. 183–91.

to produce evidence rebutting an inference of bad character would be convicted. Even in the second half of the 18th Century, when urbanisation was developing apace,[50] it is crucial to realise that levels of mobility were still relatively low, while media of communication through the rapidly developing press, along with rising literacy rates, allowed for the diffusion of advertisements and the pursuit of offenders across strikingly large areas.[51] John Fielding, the influential mid-century London magistrate and reformer, used this to good advantage by instituting a system of sending descriptions of suspected offenders wanted in London as far afield as the North East, from which records show that a significant number of suspects were returned.[52]

To today's criminal lawyer, beyond its highly discretionary nature and the spectacular features of the 'Bloody Code' which threatened (though much more rarely exacted) the death penalty for a vast range of even minor property offences, perhaps the most striking aspect of the 18th Century criminal process was the fact that it appears to have operated quite effectively without anything approaching the technical doctrines of responsibility-attribution which form the backbone of criminal law today. Today, the state's responsibility to prove not only criminal conduct but individual responsibility for that conduct lies at the heart of criminal law's legitimation as a system of justice rather than one of sheer force: the fairness of criminalisation and punishment is fundamentally premised on the idea that an offender's capacities of understanding, awareness and self-control were engaged at the time of the alleged offence. In the 18th Century, by contrast, though culpability requirements such as having acted 'maliciously', 'wickedly', 'feloniously' or '*animus furandi*' had long been discussed by commentators and asserted by judges as aspects of many common law offences, notably murder and theft, these were very far from equating to the

---

[50] On urbanisation in the 18th Century, see Watt, *The Rise of the Novel* op. cit. pp. 177–91; G.J. Barker-Benfield, *The Culture of Sensibility: Sex and Society in Eighteenth-Century England* (University of Chicago Press 1996).

[51] The classic text on literacy and reading is Richard D. Altick's *The Common Reader: A Social History of the Mass Reading Public 1800–1900* (University of Chicago Press 1957): contrary to the implication of its subtitle, the book considers the growth of literacy well before the 19th Century. See also Watt, *The Rise of the Novel* op. cit. Chapter II.

[52] Morgan and Rushton, *Rogues, Thieves and the Rule of Law* op. cit. Chapter 2.

psychological and capacity-based requirements of '*mens rea*' with which we are familiar today.

Social institutions like criminal law require, as Stephen Shapin has put it, 'sources and grounds of legitimacy: every institution needs a bit of culture that testifies to "its rightness in reason and in nature"'.[53] So the lack in the 18ᵗʰ Century of what is central to legitimation in contemporary criminal law is significant. It is always tempting, as John Baker noted,[54] to 'read the past backwards', and many modern commentators have assumed that '*mens rea*' is already an archetypal feature of English criminal law by this period. But there are both practical and conceptual reasons to question this assumption. First, in the light of the features already mentioned—speed of trial, lack of legal argumentation, predominance of lay justice—it seems unlikely that the run-of-the-mill 18ᵗʰ Century trial process could have managed evidence of '*mens rea*' in the modern, psychological, capacity-based sense as a formal object of proof. Second, and more fundamentally, as Jeremy Horder has argued, features of early modern criminal law such as the 'malice principle', though already subject to technical analysis in legal treatises, operated in significantly different ways from modern notions of '*mens rea*', and invited not the finding of a 'state of mind' but rather a non-dualistic evaluation of the conduct in question founded in what George Fletcher has called a 'pattern of manifest criminality'.[55] Ideas of '*mens rea*' developed over a long period of time, and much of the conceptual groundwork was laid across the terrain of criminal defences. But it is important to note that long-standing defences which would today be interpreted in largely psychological terms, and which even abut on mental incapacity defences, had a very different meaning in their original context. The classic example here, as Horder's important study

[53] Stephen Shapin, *A Social History of Truth: Civility and Science in Seventeenth-Century England* (University of Chicago Press 1994), quoting Mary Douglas, *How Institutions Think* (Syracuse: Syracuse University Press 1986) p. 55.

[54] *The Law's Two Bodies* p. 84.

[55] See Jeremy Horder, 'Two Histories and Four Hidden Principles of Mens Rea' 113 *Law Quarterly Review* (1997) 95; see also Gerald Leonard, 'Towards a Legal History of American Criminal Theory: Culture and Doctrine from Blackstone to the Model Penal Code' 6 *Buffalo Criminal Law Review* (2003) 691–832; Guyora Binder, 'The Rhetoric of Motive and Intent' *Buffalo Criminal Law Review* (2002) 1–96 at pp. 15–27; George P. Fletcher, *Rethinking Criminal Law* (Boston and Toronto: Little Brown 1978). The concept of manifest criminality is discussed in more detail below.

revealed, is that of provocation, which in early modern criminal law constituted not an excuse based on loss of self-control but a partial justification for homicide which was rooted in a distinctively gendered system of honour.[56] In the next section, I shall argue that commentators' mis-reading of early modern legal concepts derives from a failure to appreciate not only the distinctive legal/conceptual framework illuminated by Horder, but also the fact that this framework itself proceeded from a highly distinctive world-view.

How, then, did the early modern system of responsibility-attribution work? Beyond a baseline assumption of capacity (which could be displaced by evidence of manifest insanity), the trial was firmly focused not on *internal* questions about the defendant's state of mind but rather on the *external* 'facts of the matter'. Where evidence about conduct was questionable, the patterns of attribution based on local knowledge about character and reputation which dominated the pre-trial process also informed the trial itself. In effect, a judgment of criminal responsibility was a judgment of bad character—or, perhaps more accurately, proceeded on the basis of a default assumption of bad character which could on occasion be rebutted by convincing evidence of good character.[57] The legitimation of the 18th Century criminal trial rested fundamentally in this grounding in common sense evaluations: this was what provided its 'rightness in reason and nature'. Hence the need for the jury to assess the defendant's credibility as a witness in a direct and unmediated way was at the core of the resistance to allowing representation by counsel. Most 18th Century criminal trials were not driven primarily

---

[56] Jeremy Horder, *Provocation and Responsibility* (Oxford: Clarendon Press 1992)

[57] See Nicola Lacey, 'Character, Capacity, Outcome: Towards a framework for assessing the shifting pattern of criminal responsibility in modern English law', in Markus Dubber and Lindsay Farmer (eds.), *Modern Histories of Crime and Punishment* (Stanford University Press 2007) pp. 14–41; on the pervasiveness of character evidence in the 18th Century, see also Joel Peter Eigen, *Witnessing Insanity* op. cit. pp. 11, 14; Dana Rabin, *Identity, Crime and Legal Responsibility* op. cit. pp. 3, 31–3, 51, 85, 120, 160; Jan-Melissa Schramm, *Testimony and Advocacy in Victorian Law, Literature and Theology* op. cit. pp. 67–82; Bruce Smith, 'The Presumption of Guilt in the English Law of Theft' op. cit. p. 7; and on its persistence in the 19th Century, Lisa Rodensky, *The Crime in Mind: Criminal Responsibility and the Victorian Novel* op. cit. pp. 44–7. As Langbein notes, even in the very serious cases reported in the *State Trials*, Stephen notes that evidence of bad character operated to raise a presumption of guilt (*The Origins of Adversary Criminal Trial* op. cit. pp. 190–1).

by criminal law: rather, they involved a very human process of judgment, shaped by prevailing cultural assumptions about guilt and innocence, good and evil, sanity and madness, credibility and unreliability. Notwithstanding the radical reconstruction of the criminal process in the first half of the 19th Century—the abolition of many of the capital statutes, the creation of the police, the consolidation of the law of evidence and so on—the legal doctrine of capacity-based individual responsibility as an object of proof in the court room was still developing right through to the mid-20th Century—a much slower process than has been assumed by many historians of criminal law.[58]

The treatment of what we would today call mental incapacity defences is particularly instructive here, for it illustrates that even when matters of mental capacity were before 18th Century criminal courts, their handling was very different from that which a modern lawyer might expect. Though rules excluding the testimony of witnesses on grounds of incompetency were already developing in the 18th Century,[59] there was no statutory recognition of an insanity defence until 1800, and no elaborated common law definition of insanity until the McNaghten rules were formulated in 1843.[60] Of course—as remains the case today—many potential insanity cases would have been filtered out of the criminal process long before they came to trial. But, as records show, significant numbers of putatively insane defendants nevertheless reached the courts: Joel Peter Eigen has identified 331 cases before the Old Bailey between 1760 and 1843 in which issues of mental derangement were raised as possible defences.[61] And when such cases did reach the courts, their disposal was shaped by common-sense jury assumptions about madness and its implications for the vicious will which underpinned culpability. That there is little sign of any analysis of the definitions of insanity discussed by treatise writers like Hale or Blackstone in most of the run-of-the-mill

---

[58] See for example K.J.M. Smith, *Lawyers, Legislators and Theorists* (Oxford: Clarendon Press 1998).

[59] See Elizabeth P. Judge, *Character Witnesses: Credibility and Testimony in the Eighteenth Century Novel* (D.Phil. thesis, Dalhousie University 2004, Chapter 4).

[60] *M'Naghten's Case* 10 *Clarke and Finnelly* (1843) 200.

[61] Joel Peter Eigen, *Witnessing Insanity*, op. cit. p. 6; the annual rate grew slowly from 33 in the 1760s to 71 in the 1830s, by which time the insanity defence had already undergone some formalisation. The overall rate, however, was low, amounting to between 4 and 8 cases per 1000.

cases reported in the Proceedings of the Old Bailey should come as
no surprise given the usual absence of defence lawyers. And while
medical testimony was gradually emerging as a relevant matter, it
was in its early forms itself closely articulated with various forms
of lay knowledge and understanding, as indeed was to be expected
in an era in which the formal organisation of the medical profession was far from having gained a monopoly over broadly medical
practice.[62]

The resulting, non-technical process of evaluation is reflected
in some very matter of fact reports. In 1710, 'Mary Bradshaw alias
Seymour, of St. Giles's without Cripplegate was indicted for feloniously stealing 2 Stuff Gowns, Value 20 s. a Stuff Petticoat 3 s. with
other things, the Goods of Elizabeth Morgan. A Cloth Petticoat
5 s. a Stuff Peticoat 3 s. 3 Dowlace Smocks 15 s. the Goods of
Anne Downing. The Fact was plainly prov'd upon the Prisoner;
but sufficient Proof being given in Court that she was an Idiot,
the Jury acquitted her.'[63] Even where the charges were much more
serious, a similar tone prevails, as in the case of Susannah Jones,
charged in 1740 with the murder of a child: 'Samuel Tuttle gave
the same Account, and added, that the Prisoner told him, she
thought somebody spoke to her, and bid her do it; and that she
acknowledg'd, she took the Child out of the Cradle with an Intent
to kill it, but having some Remorse, she laid it down again; but in
a few Minutes it crying vehemently, she took it up again, and cut
it's Throat with the Razor, which she afterwards laid in the Corner
of the Window. Her Confession (to this Purpose) before Colonel
De Veil, was read in Court, but Anthony Benn and Robert Benn,
giving the Prisoner the Character of a sober, well-behav'd Girl,
not addicted to Cruelty; and Elizabeth Sanders speaking to some
Symptoms of a disorder'd Mind in the Prisoner, the Jury acquitted
her, and found her Lunatick.'[64]

---

[62] Eigen, ibid, Chapters 4–6. see also Arlie Loughhan, *Mental Incapacity Defences
in Criminal Law* (Ph.D. thesis, London School of Economics, 2008).

[63] Old Bailey Sessions Papers, t17101206–22, 17 December 1710.

[64] Old Bailey Sessions Papers, t17400116–49, 16 January 1740; cf the case of
'Elizabeth Collins, widow…indicted for stealing one shagreen case, value 2 s.
12 knives with silver handles, value 10 s. and 12 forks with silver handles, value
6 s. the property of Henry Crow, doctor in physic, August 28. The prisoner's
behaviour at the bar, and while in confinement, as appeared by Mr. Akerman's
servants, discovered her to be insane.' (Old Bailey Sessions Papers t17660903–7).
Like about half of those raising insanity defences, she was acquitted.

This is not to say that juries or witnesses were undiscerning. One witness in the case of Elizabeth White, tried for theft in 1745, commented, 'She is more politick than mad. She is more knave than fool.'[65] White was duly convicted. As Arlie Loughnan has argued,[66] the prevailing pattern here—echoing George Fletcher's famous notion of 'manifest criminality'[67]—was a pattern of 'manifest madness': insanity was simply what a jury recognised as such. Fielding, an early advocate of modernisation and systematisation in criminal justice, was quick to satirise the indeterminacy which must occasionally have resulted. In *Tom Jones*, he comments 'Who knows what may be sufficient evidence of madness to a jury?... Madness was sometimes a difficult matter for a jury to decide; for I remember...I was once present at trial of madness, where twenty witnesses swore that the person was as mad as a march hare; and twenty others that he was as much in his senses as any man in England...'[68] But if such intractable disagreements had often troubled 18th Century juries, it seems likely that pressure for change would have come far sooner than it did.

In this rather fluid legal context, as Dana Rabin has shown in a fascinating recent book, prevailing cultural influences had a decisive and direct effect upon legal practices.[69] She marshalls evidence that the emerging culture of sensibility in the latter part of the 18th Century prompted defendants to push the boundaries of what had conventionally been understood as insanity to embrace a wide variety of states of emotional distress, gradually introducing into the courtroom a mind-body distinction which was quite new. This process was ultimately seen as threatening to the integrity of the law's prohibitions, and was accordingly closed off through the increasingly technical specification of the conditions for the insanity defence being developed in case law from the early 19th Century

---

[65] Old Bailey Sessions Papers t17451016-5, 16 October 1745.

[66] Arlie Loughnan, 'Manifest Madness: Towards a New Understanding of the Insanity Defence' 70 *Modern Law Review* (2007) 379–401; see also Roger Smith, *Trial by Medicine: Insanity and Responsibility in Victorian Trials* (Edinburgh University Press 1981), Chapter 7 of which illustrates that even in the 19th Century, non-technical assumptions about female insanity continued to inform the trial process, with infanticide cases in particular often tried without medical evidence being led.

[67] *Rethinking Criminal Law* (Boston and Toronto: Little, Brown, 1978).

[68] *Tom Jones* op. cit. pp. 562–3.

[69] *Identity, Crime and Legal Responsibility* op. cit. Chapter 3.

on. As Rabin also notes, the 18th Century cases often display what is to our eyes a strange blurring of the concepts of criminal intention and character: indeed, the idea that intent simply *was* a matter of character underpinned the 17th Century willingness to contemplate poverty as an excuse for crime.[70] Not until a case in the Old Bailey Sessions Papers of 1787 does Rabin's sample of mental incapacity cases feature a decisive judicial attempt to separate, analytically, the question of character from that of mental state.[71]

The operative assumption, I would argue, was that the defendant's conduct exhibited or expressed bad character: this was a holistic judgment of wrongful conduct and dangerousness rather than today's supposed analytical separation of (external) conduct from (internal) '*mens rea*'. The trial afforded the defendant the opportunity exculpating him- or herself—and indeed it was out of these developing arguments about defences that the elaborated doctrine of responsibility as something which had to be proven for inculpation eventually emerged in the latter half of the 19th Century. Meanwhile, the key variable in most criminal trials was the defendant's capacity to gather together credible people willing to speak for her and back up her testimony. Even when the defendant's mental state was unavoidably at issue, attributions of responsibility were based, in short, on judgments about the quality of character displayed in conduct, rather than on a careful investigation of whether the defendant's cognitive and volitional capacities were fully engaged in the relevant action.

'Character' and Judgment in Modern Social Practice: Philosophy, Law and Literature

In the age of Moll Flanders, then, the mechanisms of criminal responsibility attribution rested primarily on the evaluation of character as manifested in conduct rather than on the investigation

---

[70] Ibid pp. 87–9.
[71] Ibid p. 160: the case is that of Francis Parr, Old Bailey Sessions Papers t17870115-1. For an early example, see the judgment of Chief Justice Holt in *Margridge Kel* (1707) 119; my point, however, is that such examples were isolated. I am grateful to Jeremy Horder for alerting me to this case.

of engaged volitional and cognitive capacity. This was a world whose conception of criminal responsibility was much closer to George Fletcher's 'manifest pattern of criminality', in which crime is conceived as that which can readily and generally be identified as dangerous or threatening to the community, than to his 'subjective pattern', in which the essence of criminality lies in the subjective mental state of the offender.[72] The basic institutional mechanisms which would be needed to render subjective, capacity-based responsibility an object of proof in a criminal trial were not yet in place: nor was the lack of them yet felt to be a pressing practical, political or ethical problem in a world which had yet to complete Maine's famous move from 'status to contract'. But this world was beginning to change; and the 'long 18th Century' from the Restoration in 1660 to the First Reform Act of 1832 saw the gradual assembly of many of the doctrines and institutional arrangements which we take for granted as features of criminal law and criminal justice today: the rise of an autonomous and organised legal profession with the right to represent defendants across the whole spectrum of criminal cases; the establishment of the police; systematic law reporting; a developed law of evidence; and an elaborated set of legal principles governing the attribution of criminal responsibility. How did these developments come about? And why?

In pursuing these questions, I now need to distinguish between two levels of analysis which so far have been running in parallel in the course of my argument. I hope to have established a strong case for the view that criminal responsibility understood in the internal, capacity-based sense we understand it in today could not have functioned across the vast bulk of the 18th Century criminal process because the relevant institutional mechanisms for its investigation were lacking. But this argument would be perfectly consistent with the proposition that the basic conception of responsibility in play in early 18th Century England—along with closely associated ideas such as subjecthood, individuality, agency and identity—was just the same as our modern conception, and that it merely took some time to assemble the practical forum in which to make that conception legally operational. So is what we are talking about here a fundamental conceptual shift, or rather a shift in institutional mechanisms of judgment? And can concepts

---

[72] *Rethinking Criminal Law* op. cit.

such as 'selfhood' or 'responsibility' be understood independently of the institutional practices through which they are enacted? That ideas of responsibility can themselves shift is clearly reflected in the fact that in the Middle Ages it was thought perfectly sensible to try, convict and punish animals—a practice which persisted in some parts of Europe up to the 19th Century.[73] I now want to focus on these broader questions in the related histories of ideas and social practices, and to suggest some reasons for thinking that the development of legal mechanisms of responsibility-attribution from a pattern based on evaluation of externally manifested character to one based on investigation of internally engaged capacity was itself a product of some much broader and deeper rethinking of the relations between self and society from the mid-17th Century onwards. In pursuing this argument, I want to set my initial argument within the context of three broad hypotheses developed by scholars in intellectual, social and literary history, each tracking a move from what we might call 'external' to 'internal' mechanisms of judgment, and each, I shall argue, mapping helpfully onto my thesis about a trajectory from character- to capacity-based responsibility attributions in criminal law.[74]

Shifting practices of selfhood

In his magisterial investigation of the philosophical origins of modern conceptions of selfhood,[75] Charles Taylor has shown how the key elements of modern individual selfhood—most notably for our purposes the idea of selfhood as involving a sense of 'inwardness' which generates the distinction between subject and object and the reflexivity of human beings as self-interpreting creatures—were assembled, gradually and unevenly, over many centuries from Aristotle on, with particularly marked developments associated with Augustine, with Descartes' Cogito, and with

[73] E.P. Evans, *The Criminal Prosecution and Capital Punishment of Animals* (London: Heinemann 1906, Faber 1987).
[74] This movement from external to internal might also be applied to developments in punishment, as famously argued by Foucault in his diagnosis of a trajectory from spectacular 'punishment of the body' to disciplinary 'punishment of the soul': Michel Foucault, *Discipline and Punish: The Birth of the Prison* (transl. Alan Sheridan, London: Allen Lane 1977).
[75] *Sources of the Self* op. cit.

Locke's sensational psychology.[76] Glimpses of the idea of a reflexive human selfhood focused on its own interior are, of course, visible in Shakespeare's plays, in Michel de Montaigne's essays, and innumerable diaries and letters of the early modern period.[77] But, Taylor argues, its conceptual contours continued to develop up to the philosophies of the Enlightenment and indeed beyond, with our understanding of what it is to be a self further shaped by the later developments of romanticism and, we might add, psychoanalysis and existentialism.

While his insight into the historical specificity of ideas of selfhood is of huge importance, Taylor focused his attention exclusively on their development within philosophical texts—a focus which, as he himself acknowledged, left out of the picture any assessment of the social and cultural institutions within which ideas of selfhood are played out, and which are needed to stabilise and co-ordinate them and indeed to make them liveable.[78] More recently, in a remarkable book which takes Taylor's analysis as its starting point, social historian Dror Wahrman has investigated this cultural and institutional context of modern selfhood, analysing the 'making of the modern self' through a mesmerising array of social practices ranging from beekeeping manuals to novels,

[76] Taylor's is not a radically relativist position: in his account, core aspects of selfhood are already in place in ancient Greek philosophy and are in a process of development from this core across the centuries: hence the fact that figures like Moll Flanders are readily recognisable to modern readers: Taylor, ibid. Chapter 12.

[77] As Lionel Trilling famously observed in his classic study, *Sincerity and Authenticity* (Cambridge: Harvard University Press 1972). In tracing a broad move from sincerity to authenticity as the key mark of selfhood, Trilling's main focus, like Taylor's, is on philosophical and literary sources rather than a broader range of social institutions. In tracing the emergence of ideas of authenticity, he gives particular emphasis to Rousseau.

[78] More recently, Taylor has addressed the broader conditions under which ideas, or 'social imaginaries', can be realised in terms of the notion of 'repertories': 'We can think of the social imaginary of a people at a given time as a kind of repertory...including the ensemble of practices they can make sense of. To transform society according to a new principle of legitimacy, we have to have a repertory that includes ways of meeting this principle. This requirement can be broken down into two facets: (1) the actors have to know what to do, have to have practices in their repertory that put the new order into effect; and (2) the ensemble of actors have to agree on what these practices are.'; *Modern Social Imaginaries* (Durham: Duke University Press 2004) p. 115. I am grateful to Moira Gatens for drawing my attention to this argument.

via theatre, fashion, portraiture and translations of the classics.[79] Focusing mainly on the 18th Century, Wahrman argues that the Enlightenment philosophies of the 17th Century—notably Locke's notion of the individual as *tabula rasa* to be shaped by experience, and the decline of faith in a more essential notion of human nature and relation to authority located in a divinely ordered universe—gave birth to a new and distinctively fluid conception and social practice of identity.[80] This Wahrman calls—somewhat confusingly, since it is in fact new to the Enlightenment period on his argument—the '*ancien régime* of identity'. The primary feature of this notion of selfhood was that identity was something which was socially produced and which had to be created and assumed: as a social construct, it was changeable, and could be adapted through the adoption of different clothes, different manners, different associates, different forms of comportment.[81]

In the 1780s, for complex reasons which are beyond our scope here,[82] this external, social, constructed notion of selfhood,

---

[79] *The Making of the Modern Self* (Yale University Press 2004). For other important works historicising selfhood, and exploring the conditions under which emerging ideas of selfhood operate and by which they are enabled, see variously Roy Porter (ed.), *Rewriting the Self: Histories from the Renaissance to the Present* (London and New York: Routledge 1997); Richard Sennett, *The Fall of Public Man* (London: Faber 1977); Patricia Meyer Spacks, *Imagining a Self: Autobiography and Novel in Eighteenth Century England* (Cambridge, MA: Harvard University Press 1976); Nikolas Rose, *Governing the Soul: The Shaping of the Private Self* (first published 1989; 2nd ed, London and New York: Free Association Books 1999); Lynn Hunt, *Inventing Human Rights: A History* (New York: W.W. Norton 2007).

[80] On the resonance between the 'forensic' Lockean concept of selfhood and modern commercial society, see also Ian Hacking, *Rewriting the Soul: Multiple Personality and the Sciences of Memory* (Princeton University Press 1995) pp. 146–7.

[81] Wahrman's account has much in common with Stephen Shapin's persuasive analysis of the way in which, in 17th Century England, the *making* of an identity—a collective as much as an individual project, and one which drew on available cultural resources so as to maximise the credibility of authorship—underpinned the acceptance of new claims in what we would now call the natural sciences: *A Social History of Truth* op. cit. Chapters 3 and 4.

[82] Wahrman's explanation centres on cultural anxieties about identity attendant on the American war of independence. His account of the fall of the '*ancien régime* of identity' has much in common with Richard Sennett's account of 'public man', a *persona* founded in norms of public sociability, which gives way by the 19th Century in Sennett's account to a notion founded in authenticity, itself implying a gulf between manifestation and interior selfhood (*The Fall of Public Man* op. cit.). There is also a strong resonance here with Lionel Trilling's argument in *Sincerity and Authenticity* op. cit.; while sincerity, like *ancien régime*

epitomised by the social institution of the masquerade,[83] begins to be displaced by what Wahrman dubs the 'modern regime of identity', in which individual personhood is taken to inhere in the unique and stable inner self which ultimately found perhaps its most complete expression in Romanticism. The difference between the two notions of identity is nicely evoked in their respective views of the nature of childhood: in the *ancien régime*, the child is a *tabula rasa*, whose later self is shaped by education and environment; in the modern regime, in Wordsworth's famous phrase, 'the child is father of the man', and social institutions such as education must concentrate on eliciting and perfecting that inner and stable essence rather than on tutoring a basically malleable subject. While for the *ancien régime* self of Defoe's *Moll Flanders* or *Roxana*, aliases, disguises and masquerades are normal ways of constructing identity, for the modern self of William Godwin's *Caleb Williams* in 1794, the need to adopt a disguise is regarded as a painful violation of authenticity.[84]

Wahrman's conception of the *ancien régime* of identity bears close analogy with my thesis about a move from assessments of responsibility based on a reading of the externally viewable indices of character towards a practice of attribution which is fundamentally concerned to investigate the interior world of the defendant. In the pre-*ancien régime* world of fixed status, and in the *ancien régime* world of a voluntarily espoused identity, there is little reason for the legal system, or any other system of judgment, to look behind appearances, even if the institutional mechanisms for doing so had existed. Only with the modern idea of selfhood as residing in an inner depth would an investigation of the psychological interior become important to the legitimation of practices of judgment such as criminal law.

---

identity, could be enacted, and had to be learnt as a social repertoire, authenticity, like modern regime identity, is conceptually independent of its social enactment.

[83] Cf. E.J. Hundert's argument that character was regarded in the early 18th Century as an artefact founded in display and role-play, symbolised in the cultural salience of contemporary theatre: 'The European Enlightenment and the History of the Self', in Roy Porter (ed.), *Rewriting the Self* p. 72 at p. 81; in the same collection, Sylvana Tomaselli observes that the idea of selfhood as formed by the contemporary Age was next to being a commonplace in 18th Century England ('The Death and Rebirth of Character in the 18th Century', p. 84).

[84] Daniel Defoe, *Moll Flanders* (1722: op. cit.) and *Roxana or, The Fortunate mistress* (1724: Oxford World's Classics 1996); William Godwin, *Things as They Are, or, The Adventures of Caleb Williams* (Penguin Classics 1988).

But there is a further reason for us to be interested in Wahrman's argument. This has to do with the impact of the shifting regimes of identity on gender. In one of the most fascinating passages of his book, Wahrman offers an analysis of successive editions of the leading, widely read, bee-keeping manual through the 18th Century. At this time, bee-keeping was a socially and economically important practice; but the beehive also had a strong cultural significance as a metaphor for the polity and for social relations within it—as is most famously reflected in Bernard Mandeville's *Fable of the Bees* (1723). In illustration of his argument that the shift from *'ancien'* to *'modern'* notions of selfhood implied a move from something not dissimilar to Judith Butler's post-structuralist view of 'gender as performance' to an essentialist view of sex difference,[85] Wahrman cites a striking change in the manual's representation of the social world of the hive. Whereas in early 18th Century editions, the hive is represented as being under the sovereign governance of the Queen, with worker bees her ambassadors, subjects and servants, by end of the Century, the Queen has become—you have doubtless guessed it—a mother; the progenitor of the race, to be nurtured and protected by males because of her reproductive powers. It is surely no accident that Moll Flanders belongs to the world of the Queen bee as sovereign, and Wahrman in fact cites Defoe as key example of the *ancien régime* of identity, both in his writing and in his own mobile and multiple life.

Selfhood and judgment in literary realism

The second of the three broad hypotheses about a move from external to internal modes of judgment in the 18th Century which I shall examine is drawn from Ian Watt's hugely and deservedly influential *The Rise of the Novel*.[86] Watt locates the origins of the novel precisely within the emergence of modern notions of

---

[85] *Gender Trouble: Feminism and the Subversion of Identity* (New York and London: Routledge 1999). As Wahrman also notes, some of the most influential 17th and 18th Century philosophers, notably Thomas Hobbes, regarded gender as a social construct rather than a natural difference; on this point see also Stephen Shapin, *A Social History of Truth* op. cit. pp. 86–93. On 18th Century cultural frankness about sex and bodily functions, see Vic Gatrell, *City of Laughter* (London: Atlantic Books 2006).

[86] Op. cit.

individual selfhood and of the place of individuals within an emerging bourgeois and capitalist culture.[87] This was a world in which literacy and printing technology were advanced enough to make the popular form of the realist novel viable, while the location of publishing patronage with booksellers, rather than, as in France, with court elites, opened up the space for a novel genre which could explore the emerging forms of life and help people— particularly of the middling sort—to make sense of themselves in a rapidly changing world. For Watt, the rise of the novel is inextricably linked with the rise of individualism and of a sense of the importance of the individual's inner, psychic world. But he distinguishes between two forms of the early novel. The first is a 'realism of representation' typified by Daniel Defoe and Samuel Richardson. In this realism, mock-autobiographical or epistolary first person reports of characters' moment-by-moment experiences are the primary focus. This focus, Watt argues, emerges both from the protestant tradition and from the capitalist world view of non-aristocratic, trade class authors closely in touch with, and intrigued by, the emerging commercial world and the radical empiricist psychology of philosophers like Locke. As McKeon puts it, Defoe and Richardson transformed the traditions of spiritual and criminal autobiography for a capitalist age.[88]

The second form of realism is typified by Henry Fielding, and is associated with the Augustan tradition, which privileged the precedents of the classics and of Aristotelian philosophy. In this 'realism of assessment', a didactic narrator provides an ironic and sometimes straightforwardly judgmental evaluation of characters and their situations.

---

[87] Cf., in relation to a broader European tradition of fiction, Franco Moretti, *The Way of the World: The Bildungsroman in European Culture* (translated by Albert Sbragia, London: Verso 2000). There is, of course, a vigorous debate about whether the origins of English individualism are to be found in the 17th and 18th Centuries, or whether they have much longer historical roots: see Alan MacFarlane, *The Origins of English Individualism: The Family, Property and Social Transition* (Cambridge University Press 1979).

[88] McKeon, *The Origins of the English Novel 1600–1740* (Johns Hopkins University Press 1987) pp. 98, 121–2, 241–4, 317ff. Watt's 'realism of representation' has itself been divided into two sub-groups, which are sometimes argued to be gendered, with the masculine/capitalist/rationalist representations of Defoe distinct from the feminine/sentimental/emotional representations of Richardson. On Defoe's particular, casuistic genre of representation, see George. A. Starr, *Defoe and Casuistry* (Princeton University Press 1971). For further discussion of Locke's impact on novelistic conceptions of selfhood, see Sylvana Tomaselli, 'The Death and Rebirth of Character in the Eighteenth Century', op. cit. at p. 84.

Here, the advocate rather than the witness speaks; the social takes priority over the individual.[89] Individual characters are exemplars of social types rather than psychological individuals: they are, in the terms famously coined two centuries later by E.M. Forster, 'flat' rather than 'round' characters.[90] In the development of the novel in the 18th Century, so Watt argues, with the partial exceptions of Lawrence Sterne and Frances Burney, these two realisms remain relatively distinct until the arrival of Jane Austen. Her combination of an ironic yet unobtrusive narrator with an acute psychological feel for her subjects produced, Watt argues, a brilliant synthesis which resolved the main formal difficulties of the realist novel. It is clear, however, that the kernel of the novel's novelty, as it were, lies for Watt in the individualist psychological realism of Defoe and Richardson.

Teleologies are, of course, out of fashion, and Watt's argument about the development of the novel has, inevitably, been subject to criticism. Michael McKeon[91] in particular has argued persuasively for a less linear conception of the novel as negotiating, and tracing the links between, perplexing questions of truth and virtue arising out of new socio-historical conditions. Key among these conditions are secularisation and the development of a commercial society founded on possessive individualism. The novel's exploration of how to make factual and evaluative judgments in this emerging world takes a dialectical form, moving between a naïve empiricist reaction to the tradition of romance, calling forth a conservative reaction, marked by extreme scepticism, which then invites a counter-reaction. In McKeon's account, the antagonism between Richardson and Fielding symbolises not two differing types of novel form but rather this continuing dialectic about the proper criteria for both knowledge and ethical conduct—a dialectic which stretches from at least the early 17th right through to the 19th Century. While the edges of the novel and indeed of individualism are, in his view, more blurred and reach further back

[89] On the difference between Fielding and Richardson in terms of the privileging of the voices of, respectively, advocate and witness, see Schramm, *Testimony and Advocacy in Victorian Law, Literature and Theology* op. cit. p. 83.
[90] E.M. Forster, *Aspects of the Novel* (Harcourt 1927). As Watt notes, both Ford Madox Ford and Walter Scott also criticised the lack of psychological credibility of Fielding's characters.
[91] *The Origins of the English Novel 1600–1740* op. cit.

than in Watt's account, McKeon also argues that the very engage-
ment between competing conceptions of novelistic writing implies
a recognition that the various authors were engaged in the same
enterprise; and moreover that this enterprise had fundamentally to
do with teaching readers how to live as subjects in an emerging
individualist, capitalist and secular world.[92]

On the face of it, Watt's and McKeon's association of the novel
with the emergence of secularism, capitalism and individualism is in
tension with Wahrman's argument that the *ancien régime* of identity
dominated through most of the 18th Century. The two, can, however, be brought into alignment once we note two aspects of Watt's
account. First, Watt's identification of a 'realism of assessment', persisting as a distinctive and influential literary model throughout the
Century, fits well with the idea of identity as essentially social and
relational, as it does with the idea of practices of judgment or evaluation as primarily trained on the external markers of conduct, type
or role. The 'characters' people enacted, in both Wahrman's *ancien
régime* and Watt's 'realism of assessment', were the proper and final
object of evaluation. Furthermore, as Watt himself acknowledges,
the psychological individualism of neither Defoe nor Richardson is
entirely believable to the modern reader. This is not least because
the episodic nature of their particular autobiographical and epistolary forms blocks the kind of developmental perspective which is the
hallmark of the 19th Century realism, and which proceeds from an

---

[92] More recently, Watt has been criticised as 'essentialising' the novel genre
through an ahistorical interpretation: rather than a focus on changes in literary
form, Deidre Shauna Lynch has argued that attention should be paid to practices of reading, in which readers project changing needs onto literary texts: see
Lynch, *The Economy of Character: Novels, Market Culture and the Business of Inner
Meaning* (University of Chicago Press 1998) pp. 4, 6, 34, 123–4. As will be apparent from my argument, I have much sympathy with the historicising impulse
behind both McKeon's and Lynch's accounts, and I will return to discuss aspects
of their arguments in due course. But I am not persuaded that their main elements are fundamentally incompatible with Watt's account. While Lynch's argument about the importance of readers' interpretations in re/constructing literary
notions of selfhood is persuasive, it is not incompatible with Watt's thesis: the
changing culture and economy which produce new needs for readers also, after
all, shape the perspectives of writers and the literary forms which they deploy.
While Watt's thesis can be read in formal terms, he is in fact careful to historicise
his argument within an analysis of reading practices and of the emerging institutions of a capitalist economy, and the core of his argument can stand independent
of the over-neat teleological account of the novel's gradual perfection to which
Lynch and, in less stringent form, McKeon, object.

ontology much more similar to our own. Furthermore, with only the first person voice speaking to us, these novels' characters are not fully subject to assessment by and in relation to other individuals.[93] Yet more fundamentally, as Deidre Lynch has argued, what early 18th Century readers were looking for was not so much individualism in the interior, psychological sense, but rather clues about the proper forms of sociability between individuals in an increasingly commerce-driven world: 'In this context,' as she puts it, 'most talk about character was not talk about individualities or inner lives. It was talk about the systems of... fiduciary exchange—the machinery of interconnectedness—that made a commercial society go.'[94] The hectic, jerky reports of consciousness—analogously with the whirling journeys of figures such as Smollett's appropriately named *Roderick Random*[95]—reflect a sense of the unsettling implications for the continuity of identity suggested by Lockean psychology, made yet more explicit in Hume's notion of the self as fragmented, and reflected in Wahrman's *ancien régime*, while also holding up to readers models of association in an increasingly mobile world organised around an economy depending on exchanges with strangers.

So psychological individualism—along with its implications for identity—is itself subject to competing interpretations. Individualism, as Watt indeed shows and as McKeon argues in more detail,[96] did not burst onto the 18th Century world all of a piece: rather, it was in a gradual process of dialectical development—by social actors, including lawyers, defendants, writers and

[93] On the deficiencies of *Moll Flanders* as a psychological novel *by 20th Century standards* see Carolyn A. Williams, 'Another Self in the Case: Gender, Marriage and the Individual in Augustan Literature', in Roy Porter (ed.), *Rewriting the Self* op. cit. p. 97 at p. 116. However, novelists in the first person tradition did create techniques which invited readers to evaluate characters' credibility to some degree: by, for example, making them report the reactions of other actors. See Thomas Keymer and Peter Sabor, *Pamela in the Marketplace: Literary Controversy and Print Culture in Eighteenth-Century Britain and Ireland* (Cambridge University Press 2005) p. 14.

[94] *The Economy of Character* op. cit. Introduction, p. 6; see more generally Chapter 2.

[95] Tobias Smollett, *The Adventures of Roderick Random* (1748: Oxford World's Classics 1979); cf. the episodic narrative of Sterne's *The Life and Opinions of Tristram Shandy, Gentleman* (1759–67: Oxford World's Classics 1998), a book whose 'postmodern' feel to today's reader gives further evidence of Wahrman's *ancien régime* of identity, yet whose combination of reported interiority and wry commentary testifies to Watt's/McKeon's notion of synthesis/dialectic.

[96] *The Origins of the English Novel* op. cit. Parts I and II.

readers—through the century. While Fielding's focus on types res-
onates with the '*ancien régime* of identity', the animating principle
of his plots up to *Amelia* (1757)—the social principle of birth—
denotes a certain fixity or determinism of character, while Defoe's
or Richardson's organising dynamic of choice and money fits better with the scheme of identity proper to the culture of both the
masquerade and early capitalism. What is at issue here is a long
process of transition, in law as in other cultural, economic and
political forms. It was a transition which inevitably produced, as
both Wahrman and Watt are discerning enough to acknowledge,
hybrids which may be distorted by too rigid an application of the
developmental hypotheses which are nonetheless of crucial importance to any macro-historical analysis.

Shifting practices of proof: credit, credibility and character

Both Wahrman's and Watt's analyses speak to what we might
call the phenomenology of modern individualism: the basic ideas
of what it is to be an individual in a social order, and hence of
how individual and social relations could, and should, be represented in novels or lived in social practices. They therefore speak
directly to the second level of our inquiry: that of whether basic
ideas of responsibility, as well as the legal institutions necessary
to their operation in criminal justice, were changing during the
18th Century. Our third hypothesis about a move from external to
internal modes of judgment occupies an intermediate position in
that it has to do not so much with phenomenology or ontology as
with epistemology: not with what is in the world, but with how
we can come to know about it.[97] In criminal justice, the move
towards a world understood in terms of the 'modern regime of
identity' or 'bourgeois individualism' might well be expected to set
up a legitimation demand for the development of ideas of individual and inwardly rooted responsibility for crime. But without an
epistemology showing how that inward basis for responsibility can
be known, and without the rules, doctrines and institutions which

---

[97] On the rise of interest in epistemology from the 17th Century, see Richard
Rorty, *Philosophy and the Mirror of Nature* (Princeton University Press 1979).

make that epistemology operational, the co-ordination role of the emerging notion of responsibility cannot be met.

At the time that Enlightenment ideas were issuing in contemporaries' ontological sense of a secular universe peopled by malleable individuals developing through their experiences, it is hardly surprising that ideas about how that universe may be apprehended or known were equally on the agenda. This focus is reflected nicely in the titles of influential contemporary philosophical tracts, notably John Locke's *An Essay Concerning Human Understanding* (1690).[98] And developments in the early phase of the natural sciences—notably in Newton's theories and in Bacon's exploration of the notion of probability—were beginning to have a marked effect on ideas about knowledge and proof which were of direct relevance to the legal process.[99] In the status-based, immobile, universally ordered world, proof could be taken on authority; if the privileged source of written evidence was missing[100]—as was typical in criminal trials—testimony could be effectively stabilised in a legal context by the invocation of divine sanction *via* the oath. And even once the decline of a religious world-view weakened the symbolic power of the oath, the evaluation of testimony was, as Jan-Melissa Schramm and Elizabeth Judge have persuasively argued,[101] stabilised within a regime of 'credit'—*i.e.* of confidence in the veracity of witnesses grounded in objectively discernible markers of status or honour such as age, gender and social caste.

In this world, assertions of truth continued to rely on markers of credibility which were strongly associated with a status society: birth, gentility and honour key among them. This, of course,

[98] (Oxford University Press 1979): cf. David Hume's *Enquiry Concerning Human Understanding* (1748: Oxford University Press 1999) and *A Treatise of Human Nature* (1739–40: Oxford University Press 2000).

[99] See Barbara Shapiro, *Probability and Certainty in Seventeenth-Century England: A Study of the Relationships between Natural Science, Religion, History, Law and Literature* op. cit.; Stephen Shapin, *A Social History of Truth: Civility and Science in Seventeenth-Century England* op. cit.

[100] Gallanis, 'The Rise of Modern Evidence Law', op. cit.

[101] See Jan-Melissa Schramm, *Testimony and Advocacy in Victorian Law, Literature and Theology* op. cit. Chapters 1–3, in particular pp. 50–62, 95–100; Elizabeth F. Judge, *Character Witnesses: Credibility and Testimony in the Eighteenth-Century English Novel* op. cit. Judge is arguing here somewhat against the grain of Barbara Shapiro's claim that assertions of status-based credit were rarely decisive even in the 17th Century ('Religion and the Law: evidence, proof and 'matter of fact', op. cit. at p. 193). Shapiro's argument, however, leaves intact the point that status was one important factor.

was equally the case well beyond the law, reaching to a variety of contexts including commercial transactions and scientific discourse. As Margot Finn puts it in her fascinating study of the ways in which allegedly 'pre-modern' indicators of personal status and social networks of trust stabilised the credit relations which were central to the development of an allegedly anonymous, contractual, capitalist economy, 'Creditors sought constantly and unsuccessfully to read debtors' personal worth and character from their clothing, their marital relations, their spending patterns and their perceived social status...Trade credit was determined not by known quantities of capital but by known qualities of character.'[102] And in the emerging natural sciences, as Stephen Shapin has shown, it was a fundamental assumption that credible *knowledge* came from credible *persons*: 'Credible knowledge was established through the practices of civility...Knowledge of who speaks [was] pervasively pertinent to decisions about whether what is spoken may be relied upon, and acted upon as true.'[103]

At this stage, hypotheses about the regime of knowledge and proof typical of 18th Century legal and social processes diverge. On the one hand, it has been argued that the impact of the natural sciences and of Baconian probability theory conduced to an increasing perception of human error and fallibility, leading to a declining trust in testimony and a corresponding increase in faith in, and reliance upon, circumstantial evidence. The painstaking accumulation of such evidence, calling out the reader's or juror's quasi-scientific powers of deduction and inference, in the context of an increasingly empiricist world-view, has been persuasively argued by Alexander Welsh to have privileged the 'strong representations' implicit in circumstantial evidence as a key component in models of proof. And this was true not only in criminal trials but also in novels—most notably Henry Fielding's *Tom Jones* (1749), which sets out evidence, piece by piece, for the patient reader's assimilation and evaluation.[104] On this view, jurors are in a comparable position to readers of texts,

---

[102] Margot C. Finn, *The Character of Credit: Personal Debt in English Culture, 1740–1914* (Cambridge University Press 2003) pp. 21, 47.
[103] *A Social History of Truth* op. cit. pp. 66, 126.
[104] Alexander Welsh, *Strong Representations: Narrative and Circumstantial Evidence in England* (Baltimore and London: Johns Hopkins University Press 1992). Welsh emphasises the ways in which both jurors and readers had to work actively to put together a coherent narrative out of accumulated evidence rather than relying on the surface level of testimony.

and the oral encounter associated with credibility and testimony is marginalised as characteristic of the world before modern science.

More recently, however, scholars have drawn attention to the fact that testimony remained central to the 18th Century criminal trial, whose main procedural tenets—notably the direct oral 'altercation' between defendant and jury, unmediated by defence counsel and facilitated by the judge—were fundamentally premised on the capacity of jurors to exercise their common sense in 'reading' witnesses' veracity.[105] Circumstantial evidence, after all, reached the jury *via* testimony.[106] Again, this was not peculiar to law: in the establishment of novel scientific claims to truth, too, the credibility of scientists' testimony was of fundamental importance, and lay in qualities many of which found their origins in the hierarchical status society which would remain in place for some time to come. As Stephen Shapin has shown, these implicit assertions of credibility were able to draw on parallel sources: birth, wealth, Christian piety, Aristotelian virtue, modest comportment, and—of key importance in the world of science—learning.[107] The independence and capacity for 'free action' which went with gentle status underpinned assumptions of disinterestedness which were key to scientific veracity (hence they were assumptions which, as Shapin notes, could not be mobilised by women of the gentle classes).[108]

The epistemological conditions under which jurors and other social actors confronted this hermeneutic challenge were, however, changing during the period. In the context of greater social and geographical mobility, the hierarchical and relatively static world of 'credit' in which external markers of social status were regarded as appropriate indicators of reliability was slowly giving way to a world in which it was recognised that reliability had to be assessed in terms of the particular capacities and dispositions of individual witnesses. Appearances, in other words, were becoming increasingly deceptive, and the world of surfaces, in which a pattern of manifest criminality was a practicable as well as legitimate framework for attributions of criminal responsibility, was on

[105] Jan-Melissa Schramm, *Testimony and Advocacy in Victorian Law, Literature and Theology* op. cit. pp. 18–22, 60–61, 108–9.
[106] So that, as Schramm puts it, 'testimony remains a means of proof': ibid p. 22.
[107] *A Social History of Truth* op. cit. Chapters 1–4.
[108] Ibid pp. 87–91.

the wane.[109] Elizabeth Judge has summed this up as a shift from
a world of 'credit' to a world of 'credibility;[110] from a world in
which individual character and disposition was taken to be indi-
cated by external and status-based markers, to one in which veracity and reliability was taken to be given by more elusive and
interior qualities and motivations. A world in which thieftakers
like Jonathan Wild could be important to a prosecution was, after
all, one in which status and reputation were unreliable indicators
of information useful to the proof of a criminal charge. Already
in 1724, we find Daniel Defoe probing the difficulty which individuals have in evaluating even their own sincerity: threatened
by a shipwreck, his courtesan heroine *Roxana* repents of her
life of wickedness, only to question her own sincerity when her
feelings of guilt melt away with the wind and rain: 'So certain
is it, that the Repentance which is brought about by the meer
Apprehensions of Death, wears off as those Apprehensions wear
off; and Death-bed Repentance, or Storm-Repentance, which is
much the same, is seldom true'.[111] If the veracity of testimony is
opaque even to individual selves, how much more troubling is the
veracity of others? In an increasingly fluid environment, jurors,
like other social actors finding their way around the confusing
world of early modern cities, had to be relied upon—and educated
in the art of—evaluating what Judge calls 'embodied credibility':
in other words, judging credibility on the basis of the evidence

[109] This is a theme which preoccupies many novels of the late 18th Century.
Key examples are to be found in the difficulties of recognition which plague
Charlotte Lennox's *The Female Quixote: or, The Adventures of Arabella* (1752:
Oxford World's Classics 1989) (discussed further in Chapter II); Tobias Smollett's
Roderick Random op. cit.; and in Frances Burney's meditations on the deceptive-
ness of appearances: see, in relation to the risk of 'respectable women' being
mistaken for prostitutes, and vice versa, *Evelina, The History of a Young Lady's
Entrance into the World* (1778: Penguin Classics 1994), and in relation to motives,
Camilla or, A Picture of Youth (1796: Oxford World's Classics 1971). In relation to
the urban context, see Sarah Fielding's *The Adventures of David Simple, Containing
an Account of his Travels Through the Cities of London and Westminster In the Search
of A Real Friend* (1744: Penguin Classics 2002); and in relation to the pitfalls of a
faith in physiognomy as a clue to character, see Thomas Mackenzie's *The Man of
Feeling* (1771: Oxford World Classics 2001) pp. 33–4, 57.
[110] *Character Witnesses* op. cit.; Schramm, in *Testimony and Advocacy in Victorian
Law, Literature and Theology* op. cit. pp. 69–72 gives a subtle account of the vary-
ing—financial, moral, reputational—inflections of the notion of credit: see also
Margot C. Finn, *The Character of Credit* op. cit.
[111] *Roxana or, The Fortunate Mistress* op. cit (the quotation is taken from
p. 128).

produced in physical encounters with witnesses through close observation of their words, demeanour, body language and so on. Again, there are close analogies here between law and modern science which, however emphatic its claims that knowledge must be based in direct experience rather than authority, still had to rely in practice on the credibility of truth claims. Hence both treatises of evidence and works of 'natural philosophy' gradually developed flexible 'prudential maxims' for assessing credibility: the plausibility and number of sources; the consistency of testimony; the immediacy of the evidence; the expertise of the speaker; the comportment with which a witness gave testimony; the integrity and disinterestedness of the witness.[112] External signs remained important; but, conceptually, a split was emerging between character and credibility.

Though the periodisation differs somewhat, this argument about the move from a world of credit to one of credibility maps neatly onto Wahrman's notion of the social, external nature of *ancien régime* identity as giving way to a modern regime of fixed selfhood located in the psychological interior. As urbanisation and commerce proceeded apace, the fluidity of the emerging *ancien régime* of identity posed huge interpretive challenges not only for legal decision makers like jurors but also for participants at masquerades or wanderers in the anonymised pleasure gardens and theatres of early 18th Century London. Hence there developed an increasing perplexity about how to evaluate credibility, and a corresponding fascination with the processes through which such evaluations could be made: a fascination which is reflected not only in the plots of novels like *Evelina* (1778) and *David Simple* (1744) but also in the architecture of courtrooms and the visual representation of trials, in which the jurors are placed in a prominent position, and are as frequently an object of interested observation as is the defendant.

Note, too, that this continued reliance on testimony is perfectly consistent with an important role for circumstantial evidence, the potential unreliability of which is itself pondered in novels such as *Tom Jones* and

---

[112] See Shapin (*A Social History of Truth* op. cit. Chapter 5). As he repeatedly points out, the sceptical stance articulated in much natural philosophy of the 17th Century—that the only good proof came from direct experience—was, and remains, utterly incapable of sustaining actual scientific practice.

Caleb Williams:[113] since inferences from such evidence were inevitably fallible, as Schramm puts it 'the idea that circumstances cannot lie was not so much a sophisticated rhetorical tool as a naïve epistemological confidence in the reality of appearances'.[114] It is further important to note that the collapse of the world of credit does not entail a collapse of reliance on external markers of credibility: even if that credibility is beginning to be conceived as located in the psychological interior of the modern regime of identity, social institutions may take some time to construct the mechanisms which allow for this interior to be assessed. Again, we can draw analogies with other areas of social practice: in the context of financial credit, as Margot Finn puts it, the 'modernising impulses' of the 18th Century were 'protracted' in nature and 'partial' in their effects: 'The slow pace, unstable trajectories and unintended consequences of cultural, social and economic changes are defining features of the character of credit in England from 1740 to 1914. Where Sir Henry Maine saw a modern transition from status to contract, the history of personal debts and credits reveals instead an ongoing dialogue and accommodation between contractual behaviours and the enduring status differentials of gender and of class.'[115] As I shall argue in the next chapter, there is strong reason to think that precisely the same was true in the criminal courts, with the 18th and even 19th Century marking a period of transition from the status-based world of credit to a more psychological assessment of credibility *via* an interim reliance on external markers of reputation.

Why Novels?

In the remainder of this book, I shall follow Wahrman, Welsh and others in exploring the development of social and legal ideas about

[113] As Gladfelder points out, despite the construction of *Tom Jones* around circumstantial evidence noted by Welsh (*Strong Representations* op. cit.), the plot also turns on the way in which such evidence can be misleading. Fielding himself in later life pondered the fallibility of circumstantial evidence, itself often a product of testimony, and published several essays on cases which he had tried in which apparently decisive circumstantial evidence was later discovered to have been deceptive: see *Criminality and Narrative* op. cit. Chapter 10; see also David Punter, 'Fictional Representation of Law in the 18th Century' 16 *Eighteenth-Century Studies* (1982) 47–74.
[114] Schramm, *Testimony and Advocacy in Victorian Law, Literature and Theology* op. cit. p. 59.
[115] *The Character of Credit* op. cit. p. 327.

subjecthood, responsibility and proof or attribution of responsibility by juxtaposing materials from law and other social practices, and in particular by drawing analogies between the development of these ideas in the criminal process and in the emerging genre of the novel. What justifies this reliance on the novel in particular as an index of the changes in social practices contributing to the criminalisation?

While, as several recent scholars have demonstrated, a startling range of artistic practices—caricatures, translations, theatrical productions—can give us clues to the cultural context in which the law operated and developed, there are several reasons for regarding the novel as a particularly fruitful object of analysis. First, over these two centuries we have, at just the same time as a period of rapid social change and institutional innovation in criminal justice, the rapid development of literary fiction which aspires to 'realism': indeed, as Watt argues,[116] the novel's realism is both a product of its social context and its distinctive marker in formal terms.[117] This realism is, of course—as the arguments

---

[116] *The Rise of the Novel* Chapters I and II.

[117] Of course, realist novels are members of a genre which has been retrospectively constructed by literary critics, and one with boundaries which are less than clearly demarcated between realism 'proper' and related genres. Nor did 'realism' take the same form across this long period: the classics of 19th Century realism, perhaps epitomised by George Eliot's *Middlemarch* (1871–2: Penguin Classics 1994), are of a different order from the more formulaic narratives of Defoe's and Richardson's inchoately psychological first person representative realism, of Smollett or Burney, or of Fielding's Augustan 'realism of assessment', just as Thackeray's epic realism of types in *Vanity Fair* differs from Romanticism or from the more deeply psychological individualism of George Eliot. And yet—as the protestations of many of the earlier authors, including Defoe, Richardson and Fielding, show—there was in all these works an ambition to represent or write from life. (See for example Samuel Richardson, *Pamela* (1740: Penguin Classics 1985), Richardson's preface, p. xx; Henry Fielding, *Joseph Andrews* (1742: Penguin Classics 1999), p. 203; Henry Fielding, *Tom Jones* op. cit. p. 648; *Moll Flanders* and *Roxana* were written as pretended autobiographies, with frequent references by an anonymous 'editor' to the 'fact' that the style has been changed only to the limited extent necessary to aid comprehension, in the interests of authenticity.) The books which I include in my sample are all informed at some level by an aspiration to illuminate certain truths about human nature and experience and observations about social structure. In this respect, Hardy's caustic response to the public criticism (see note 10 above) which met the publication of *Tess of the d'Urbervilles* is instructive; 'I will just add that the story is sent out in all sincerity of purpose, as an attempt to give artistic form to a true sequence of things; and in respect of the book's opinions and sentiments, I would ask any too genteel reader, who cannot endure to have said what everybody nowadays thinks and feels, to remember a well-worn sentence of St. Jerome's: 'If an offense come out

of Wahrman, Watt, McKeon, Schramm and Judge amply testify—
rooted in the writers' close acquaintance with the abstract ideas
circulating in contemporary philosophy—or philosophy being
widely read at the time. These were challenging received ideas
about the nature of 'reality': about people's views of human motivations, dispositions and relation to the social world.[118] Debates
about free will *versus* determinism; about the essential goodness
or reformability—or otherwise—of human beings; about the role
of environment in producing character and conduct; about individual responsibility and autonomy; about individual psychology
and probability, surface on almost every page of these early novels.
So, quite apart from the images of criminal justice practice to be
found in the novels—particularly, of course, the novels of Henry
Fielding, who was at once one of the greatest writers and one of
the most important criminal justice commentators and reformers of
the 18th Century, and whose chronic financial problems had given
him some experience of the practice of imprisonment for debt[119]—
they are a rich source of insight into prevailing social attitudes and
mores. Nor was Fielding alone in his particular expertise in relation to criminal justice. As a sometime bankrupt and frequently
arrested secret agent, Defoe, too, had personal experience of the
other side of the legal coin.

Moreover the blurred boundaries of the novel as a genre, with
its origins in gallows speeches, Newgate narratives, journalism
and travel writing, along with Defoe's and other early novelists'

of the truth, better is it that the offense come than that the truth be concealed.'
(Explanatory Note to the First Edition, November 1891). A kernel of realism is
also to be found in many satires, comedies of manners and sensation novels. The
relevance of these different forms of realism and quasi-realism for the representation of female criminality is explored later in this section, and in Chapter III.

[118] The ideas about human nature and understanding emerging from the
Enlightenment philosophies of figures like Locke, Hume and Rousseau, along
with older ideas about character and virtue in Aristotle and Plato, as well as
Spinozist ideas about determinism, and a panoply of ideas from various Christian
traditions, are all to be found, more or less explicit, in the novels, and provide
further clues to the complex and fast-shifting cultural world in which modern
practices of criminalisation were developing.

[119] Indeed it seems likely that Fielding was detained in a bailiff's 'spung-
ing house' while he composed *Shamela* (*An Apology for the Life of Mrs Shamela
Andrews*) (1741: Penguin Classics 1999); see Thomas Keymer and Peter Sabor,
*Pamela in the Marketplace: Literary Controversy and Print Culture in Eighteenth-
Century Britain and Ireland* op. cit. p. 15; Margot C. Finn, *The Character of Credit*
op. cit. p. 53.

practice of combining fiction with other genres of writing including fake criminal autobiography, pamphlets and political tracts, adds to the plausibility of taking novels as windows—albeit partial windows—onto the world of criminal justice.[120] Novels are, of course, a different genre from case reports such as the Old Bailey Sessions Papers; authors of both novels and reports make choices about how to present character and circumstance, but the aesthetic and professional considerations which shape those choices are significantly different. Yet even beyond the criminal justice expertise or experience of several of the most influential writers of fiction, there is more general reason to think that the social attitudes reflected in the realist novels were of decisive importance to the conduct of criminal justice in the 18th and early 19th Centuries. This is because the system—if indeed it is aptly characterised as such—was still largely administered, as we saw earlier, not by professional criminal justice officials and lawyers but by ordinary citizens in their roles as Justices of the Peace, parish constables and people bringing prosecutions or testifying about offences—many of them drawn from the middling classes who were prime consumers of the novel.

Added to the realist aspiration of the novel as an emerging genre and the experience of and interest in the criminal process of significant practitioners of the 18th Century novel, we have, second, the perhaps unsurprising fact that, as one literary critic has put it, 18th Century novels are 'obsessed with law'.[121] Real and mock trials, meditations on issues of proof, stereotypes of lawyers and legal argumentation, coruscating critiques of contemporary criminal justice and observations of the impact of criminal law on characters' lives pervade literary fiction of both 18th and early 19th

---

[120] Kieran Dolin concludes from these origins of the novel that 'the legal problem of crime proved integral to the development of the novel and helped shape literary history' (*A Critical Introduction to Law and Literature* op. cit. p. 101). Gladfelder has shown in detail how the novel grew out of other cultural representations of crime such as 'low' literature of criminal biography, Newgate Ordinaries' accounts, early lay-oriented law reports and broadsheets. For Defoe there is a particularly clear link in that he wrote many examples of the pamphlets and fake autobiographies himself. For an extensive analysis of the forms of writing from which what we now think of as novels grew, see J. Paul Hunter, *Before Novels* op. cit. On the impact of growing literacy and the demography of 18th Century reading, see Hunter, ibid. Chapter 3; Watt, *The Rise of the Novel* op. cit. Chapter II.
[121] David Punter, 'Fictional Representation of Law in the 18th Century' op. cit.

Centuries.[122] This pervasive interest in legal forms, institutions and experiences should come as no surprise, perhaps, in a secularising world in which a decline in religion and confusion about political authority had led to the emergence of law as the dominant form of temporal order.[123]

Third, it is generally accepted—and indeed utterly obvious to anyone reading early novels—that the novel as a genre had a didactic purpose, and one which was crucial to its need to differentiate itself from both the older tradition of romance and from other forms of 'low' literature. Early novels are often framed around prefaces or chapter introductions which announce this moral or educational purpose, while the invention of the third person narrator provided a new opportunity for the more or less subtle propagation of the novel's didactic role. The moral purpose of the novel was a subject of explicit debate among contemporaries, not only in the pages and prefaces of novels themselves, but in journals such as *The Rambler* and *The Lounger*.[124] Furthermore, the moral aspirations of late 18th Century novels, organised as

---

[122] It is in fact hard to think of 18th Century novels which do *not* include significant legal elements: but to take just a few examples of the preoccupation with law as central to fictional plots, think of Defoe's *Moll Flanders* (theft); *Roxana* (marriage and its legal implications); Jonathan Swift's *Gulliver's Travels* (1726: Penguin Classics 2001) (reliance on law as a sign of degeneracy of English society as compared, for example, to that of the Houhynms, and pervasive satire on lawyers' deliberate obfuscations); Smollett's *Roderick Random* (1748: op. cit.) and *Humphry Clinker* (1771: Oxford World's Classics 1998) (imprisonment for debt and suspected assault; trials and mock trials); Fielding's *Jonathan Wild* (1743: op. cit.), *Joseph Andrews* (1742: op. cit.), *Tom Jones* (1749: op. cit.) and *Amelia* (1751: Oxford: Clarendon Press 1988) (imprisonment for debt, trials and mock trials, the potential for corruption in contemporary criminal justice); Oliver Goldsmith, *The Vicar of Wakefield* (1766: Oxford World's Classics 1974) (appalling prisons, corrupt witnesses); Samuel Richardson's *Clarissa* (1747–8: Riverside Editions 1962) (rape and a woman's disinclination to subject her claim to legal investigation); William Godwin's *Caleb Williams* (1794: op. cit.) (murder, false accusation, mock trials). This preoccupation informed other salient cultural forms, too: for example, and spectacularly, both William Hogarth's prints and John Gay's *The Beggar's Opera* (1728: Penguin Classics 1986). See also John E Loftis, 'Trials and the Shaping of Identity in Tom Jones' 34 *Studies in the Novel* (2002). 1; Margot C. Finn, *The Character of Credit* op. cit. pp. 51–62.

[123] See E.P. Thompson, *Whigs and Hunters* (Harmondsworth: Penguin 1975); Gladfelder, *Criminality and Narrative* op. cit. p. 5.

[124] See, for example, Samuel Johnson's essay on 'The fiction of the present age' from *The Rambler* (31st March 1750) quoted in McKeon's *The Origins of the English Novel* op. cit. p. 414; and Thomas Mackenzie's essay 'On Novel-Writing' XX *The Lounger* (18th June 1785).

they are around conceptions of reason, proper feeling and conduct, self-mastery and respect for social order, have much in
common with those of the contemporary debate about criminal
justice reform.[125] And this intimate relationship between literary
and legal concerns persisted in the 19th Century. As Schramm has
argued, novels were importantly concerned with pondering the
implications of the supercession of 'artless' testimony as to fact
by defence counsel, whose 'artful' management of evidence in
their expanded domain after the Prisoners' Counsel Act gave rise
to significant ethical problems which were vigorously debated in
both fiction and contemporary journalism.[126] Novelists sought to
provide a space for the plain exculpatory speech of defendants
which had been silenced by the law, just as lawyers inveighed
on occasion against novelists' use of the licence which the genre
of fiction and the mechanism of an all-seeing narrator accorded
them.

In the second half of the 18th Century the genre of literary fiction had further diversified, with the creation of Gothic novels
and, later, novels of sensation and melodrama, engendering both
fragmentation of the field and some hybridity within particular
novels. In this context, it seems that the 'high' genre of classic 19th
Century realism focused on mechanisms of accusation and exculpation, while the exploration of deviance was zoned into the 'low'
genre of sensation writing.[127] Novels' cultural status remained,
throughout the 18th Century, fragile.[128] But even granting that
novels cannot be regarded as primary intellectual sources for the
development of Enlightenment thinking, their explicit attempts to
tutor their readers in social practices prescribed in those intellectual

[125] Cf. John Mullan's 'Novels and Feelings', and Carolyn D. Williams,
'Another Self in the Case: Gender, Marriage and the Individual in Augustan
Literature' op. cit. pp. 119 and 97 respectively, arguing that the novel helped—
and aimed—to fashion a self-consciousness oriented to interior selfhood.
[126] *Testimony and Advocacy in Victorian Law, Literature and Theology* op. cit. pp. 7,
9, 140–4, 180–6.
[127] See Schramm, *Testimony and Advocacy in Victorian Law, Literature and
Theology* op. cit. p. 190: I take up this issue in Chapter III. Many writers—
Dickens notable among them—exhibited features of several of the different fictional sub-genres.
[128] As reflected in the insistent attempts by novelists of the latter part of the
18th Century to assert their moral/intellectual seriousness, notably by distinguishing themselves from other traditions such as romance: see McKeon, *The Origins
of the English Novel* Part I; Lynch, *The Economy of Character* Chapter 3.

sources—the practice of interpersonal sympathy advocated by Adam Smith and David Hume, for example—qualify them as important resources in the history of the modern self;[129] indeed it renders them 'dynamic, constitute components (rather than mere reflections) of historical experience'.[130] Novels, in short, were all about exploring, and teaching their readers, how to live and interpret their surroundings—and the urgency of their mission was underscored by the rapidly changing circumstances of the world which gave them birth.

This didactic purpose of the early novel, which, for those of us brought up on a diet of later literature, is perhaps its hardest feature to digest, underpins in turn the plausibility of a cluster of persuasive arguments from literary theory about the specific educational purposes to which the novel was put. This is important for our argument, because it helps to pin down a further, more precise way in which novels are linked to legal developments. In various ways, literary scholars like Michael McKeon, Deidre Lynch and J. Paul Hunter[131] have built on Ian Watt's argument about the novel's individualist orientation to suggest that novelists were sketching not only models of appropriate conduct but also models of individual subjectivity and recognition of character from conduct, appearance and events appropriate to the emerging capitalist world. And these models were needed as much by actors in the criminal process as by readers. As McKeon argues, the gradual destabilisation of both generic categories on which knowledge had been founded, and of social categories based on status, under the pressures of commercialisation, secularisation and the impact of empiricist philosophy produced a continuing set of 'epistemological problems which themselves had a long prehistory of intense and diversified public debate'.[132] These included perplexities about how to form judgments about others and about the world, about how to negotiate and justify continuing status inconsistency, and about how to frame appropriate standards of

[129] See John Mullan, 'Feelings and Novels', in Roy Porter (ed.), *Rewriting the Self* op. cit. p. 119 at p. 126.

[130] Margot C. Finn, *The Character of Credit* op. cit. p. 3.

[131] See, respectively, *The Origins of the English Novel* (Baltimore: Johns Hopkins University Press 1987); *The Economy of Character* op. cit.; *Before Novels* op. cit. p. 46; Hunter further suggests that novels provided an emotional experience akin to a form of secular Methodism: ibid. Chapters 2 and 10–12.

[132] *The Origins of the English Novel* op. cit. p. 410.

conduct. The narrative form of the novel, he suggests, provided an appropriate forum in which to debate these issues of 'truth and 'virtue', and a context in which the question of how to live and make judgments as a possessive individual could be pondered: 'Early modern English people.... ascribed sufficient power and value to literature to regard it as political or social change "by other means". This is nowhere more obvious than in the commonplace insistence that the function of literature...is to correct and reform humankind'.[133]

John Zomchick further suggests that, in relation to the pervasive plots structured around family life and property rights, novels were propagating a new, contractual as opposed to status-based notion of the juridical subject.[134] More specifically, Elizabeth Judge has argued that novels functioned in part as guidebooks to the practice of evaluations of 'embodied credibility' authorised by contemporary philosophy and rendered necessary by legal protocols, teaching readers/jurors to assess individual veracity in a mobile world in which direct evidence of character and reputation was less often available in courtroom, theatre, pleasure garden or even drawing room.[135] In this context it is significant that many of the novelists, including Daniel Defoe and Samuel Richardson, were also authors of the conduct manuals which abounded in the world of 18th Century publishing.[136]

Fourth, and equally important to our theme, the didactic purpose of the novel as a form, combined with the fact that novels were aimed at and read, importantly if not predominantly, by women,[137] gives them a special salience in any attempt to understand changing conceptions of femininity and hence attitudes to

[133] *The Origins of the English Novel* op. cit. p. 268, see further Parts I and II, in particular pp. 144, 268–9, 334–5; 410, 416.
[134] John P. Zomchick, *Family and Law in Eighteenth Century Fiction* (Cambridge University Press 1993).
[135] Cf. Stephen Shapin's discussion of the 'prudential maxims' guiding the assessment of testimony in the natural sciences: *A Social History of Truth* op. cit. pp. 228–242.
[136] For a fascinating analysis of overlapping themes between novels and conduct books, see Naomi Tadmor, *Family and Friends in Eighteenth-Century England: Household, Kinship and Patronage* (Cambridge University Press 2001) Chapters 2 and 3. The impact of conduct books in developing gender norms is discussed in Chapter II below.
[137] See Hunter, *Before Novels*, op. cit. Chapters 2, 10–12.

female deviance.[138] Novels, certainly, had to be plausible to women:
but they also give us particularly interesting evidence—albeit evidence which requires careful interpretation—of emerging ideas
about proper norms of female conduct.[139] This makes the sudden
decline of 'ordinary' female offenders like Moll as central fictional
characters highly significant. In particular, the role of the novel
in expressing and developing the so-called 'culture of sensibility',
which will form a primary object of analysis in the next chapter, seems likely to help to explain developing attitudes to female
offending.

Finally—and perhaps most relevant to the later 18th and 19th
Centuries—novels' preoccupation with crime and deviance has
been argued by Gladfelder to have satisfied a yearning for excitement and the experience of transgression which was gradually
being marginalised in a more standardised, modern, disciplined
society—a claim which has particular plausibility when one considers the predominantly 'polite' audience for the novel.[140] There
is thus in some sense an affinity between the very project of the
novel and the transgression represented by crime. Novels respond,
in other words, to an anxiety that the pleasures of individualism
will be submerged in the social regulation and pervasive discipline
of manners which are needed to order and stabilise the modern,
capitalist, urbanised world. Around the growth of liberal individualism, ironically, there was an older form of expression of individuality which was felt to be at risk. As we shall see in the next
chapter, by the middle of the 18th Century, the carnival, the rake,
the masquerade—the marks of Wahrman's *ancien régime*—were all
under threat as impolite or dangerous. The novel, particularly in
the hands of writers like Frances Burney and Maria Edgeworth,
was at once complicit in the 'civilising' process which sought to
tame the individualist excesses invited by the *'ancien régime* of identity', while also allowing readers, through imaginative identification with characters, experiences which novels themselves held up

---

[138] Novels were, of course, also written by significant numbers of women from
Aphra Behn on: and, as we shall see in the next chapter, women writers of the
second half of the 18th Century—Frances Burney, Elizabeth Inchbald and Maria
Edgeworth key among them—were particularly concerned with other women as
the objects of their overtly didactic enterprise.
[139] Watt, *The Rise of the Novel* Chapter II; Barker-Benfield, *The Culture of
Sensibility* op. cit.
[140] Gladfelder, *Criminality and Narrative* op. cit.

to disapproval. Were novelists exploring crime or other forms of bad behaviour, Gladfelder asks, from a first person point of view, in order to rescue or enjoy this threatened experience of transgression? Is the pleasure of reading—like that of crowds at public executions—in part about identification with the deviant? And if so, is women's disappearance as fictional criminals a signal of the declining thinkability of female transgression except in certain reassuringly isolated contexts such as infanticide or crimes of passion? Or is it rather a symptom of lower levels of anxiety about women's crime?

These general themes will be taken up in the next chapter, in the light of the interlocking hypotheses already sketched about a general, slow and uneven change from the early 18ᵗʰ to the mid 19ᵗʰ Centuries in processes of social judgment, assessment and evaluation. This, I have argued, proceeded from an early confidence about reliance on external markers of status to a world in which credibility, identity and responsibility gradually came to be seen as residing in the mysterious interior world of human being. But this is to anticipate the *dénouement* of my story, and the central features of its plot now need to be set out.

CHAPTER II

'What is the use of a woman's will?': the demise of Moll in the age of sensibility

In the previous chapter, I sketched a broad thesis about mechanisms for the attribution of responsibility in 18th Century criminal justice as focused primarily on the external markers of conduct and character. I made a case for thinking that this pattern of attribution was not merely premised on the institutional imperatives of the criminal process but was articulated with a broader socio-cultural environment which was in transition between pre-modern and modern conceptions of selfhood, and which had to be understood if the legal developments were to make sense. I further suggested that there were several reasons for thinking that the genre of the novel provided a useful window on this broader environment, and one well suited to illuminating our central question about the assumptions and practices shaping the criminalisation of women. It is now time to move from the level of abstract theory and hypothesis to that of interpretation, and to put the method to work in the context of concrete legal and literary examples.

In this chapter, I aim to establish two broad propositions. First, I aim to show that while, as commentators like Rabin and Eigen have argued, the 18th Century saw a slowly emerging focus on internal markers of states of mind through the development of defences, evaluations of external markers of character remained central to the attribution of criminal responsibility right through the Century. Despite the social changes which Judge rightly saw as putting pressure on the system of 'credit', through which character was judged in terms of external markers of status, I shall argue that there is plentiful legal and literary evidence to suggest that practices of criminal judgment remained trained on character, albeit in senses which were modulating significantly over time. If, as Shapin has argued, in the more elevated world of scientific practice '"Nobility of Extraction" was a serviceable condition... [which] endowed an individual with a prior presumption of moral character that was independent of his own actions',[1] in the criminal courts, the marks of respectability operated as a similarly powerful frame shaping the interpretation of alleged conduct. In criminal justice, the 'economy of character',[2] in other words, outlived the stable, status-based world of credit for many decades—if indeed it has ever been effaced. I shall frame this argument within an analysis of criminal trials in two novels, *Joseph Andrews* and *Caleb Williams*, the former representing the powerful hold of the economy of character at mid-Century, and the latter illustrating the emerging critique of that persisting hold on the cusp of the era of criminal justice reform.

The purpose of this first argument is not merely to adjust the chronology of historical analysis. For I shall argue that it has an important upshot for our understanding of how women's agency and criminality were being constructed. Hence, second, I aim to establish that the particular 'economy of character' prevailing in the early 18th Century may have been relatively hospitable to the acknowledgment of female transgression, while developments in conceptions of the female role during the course of the Century made a decisive difference to how women's potentially criminal conduct was perceived, giving birth to a new 'economy of feminine character' which was less hospitable to the plausibility of Moll Flanders: an active and transgressive woman, the central author of her own narrative. And this in turn, I shall suggest, may help us to reconcile King's and Feeley and Little's very different analyses of female criminality over the period. I shall frame this argument within three pairings which stand for relevant developments in the literary representation of women: the

---

[1] Stephen Shapin, *A Social History of Truth* op. cit. p. 146.
[2] I borrow the phrase from Deidre Lynch: *The Economy of Character: Novels, Market Culture and the Business of Inner Meaning* op. cit.

extraordinarily rapid shift from Daniel Defoe's *Moll Flanders* to Samuel Richardson's *Clarissa* in the representation of women's proper comportment and of the consequences of their transgression; the shift from Defoe's *Roxana* to Frances Burney's *Cecilia* in the representation of women's relationship to marriage and money; and the shift from *Roxana*'s 'she-merchant' to Jane Austen's supreme home-maker, Fanny Price of *Mansfield Park*, in the representation of women's proper role.

The 'Economy of Character' in 18th Century Law and Literature: From Joseph Andrews to Caleb Williams

Character, credit and credibility

In his early novel, *Joseph Andrews* (1742),[3] Henry Fielding gives us a delicious glimpse of the 'economy of character' at work in 18th Century criminal justice—and a mordant implicit commentary on its attendant pitfalls.[4] The morally impeccable (and gloriously absent-minded) Rev. Abraham Adams and his young friend Fanny Goodwill are arraigned before a Justice for assault, in circumstances in which Adams has in fact been rescuing Fanny from sexual assault by a third party. The local Justice is keen to get matters over in highly summary fashion on the basis of the original assailant's

---

[3] Op. cit. pp. 168–70.

[4] The pitfalls are explored yet more intensively in *Jonathan Wild* op. cit. in which an extended analysis and critique of the market in character evidence is a central theme, alongside pungent satire on the distortion of the idea of 'character' in a world in which unscrupulous cunning can underpin a reputation for 'greatness of character' in both criminality and politics. As Michael McKeon has noted, Fielding's attitude to law is ambivalent: on the one hand, he is a biting critic of its failings: on the other, he is drawn to a modernising reform agenda in which law plays a leading part: *The Origins of the English Novel* op. cit. pp. 389, 401. The vulnerability of character evidence to corruption—as in the market in such evidence satirised in *Jonathan Wild*—drew attention not only from writers and practising lawyers but also from legislators: in 1792, *The Servants' Characters Act* made it an offence to impersonate a master or mistress or to give a false character reference. There were however no prosecutions under the Act until a single case in the early 20th Century: *R v Costello and Bishop* 1 *KB* [1910] 28. I am grateful to Jeremy Horder for alerting me to this legislative history.

evidently trumped up testimony: his inclination to commit Adams
to gaol, and to see 'if you can prove your Innocence at Size...'
illustrates both the functional burden of proof against the defendant and 18th Century magistrates' developing habit of committing
suspects to goal for further examination without any clear legal
mandate for so doing.[5] At this point, in Fielding's words; 'One of
the Company having looked stedfastly at Adams, asked him, 'if he
did not know Lady Booby?'. Upon which Adams presently calling
him to mind, answered in a Rapture, 'O Squire, are you there? I
believe you will inform his Worship I am innocent.' 'I can indeed
say,' replied the Squire, 'that I am very much surprised to see you
in this Situation;' and then addressing himself to the Justice, he
said, 'Sir, I assure you Mr Adams is a Clergyman as he appears, and
a Gentleman of a very good Character. I wish you would enquire a
little farther into this Affair: for I am convinced of his Innocence.';
'Nay', says the Justice, 'if he is a Gentleman, and you are sure he
is innocent, I don't desire to commit him, not I; I will commit
the woman by herself, and take your Bail for the Gentleman....'
Adams then intercedes for Fanny, is listened to, and prevails, not
least because the lying witness, seeing the turn of the tide, has
absconded.

Fielding's experience as a lawyer and, later, magistrate gave
him ample opportunity to observe the operation of criminal justice in this world in which people are confident of 'knowing a
man by his companions'.[6] But is the vignette from *Joseph Andrews*
more satire than reality? Let us compare it with the real case of
Sarah Sharp, indicted in the year of *Joseph Andrews*' publication
for the theft of 'one Pair of Stays, a Holland Apron, a black Silk
Hood, a Child's Dimity Coat, and other Things, the Property
of Robert Leake'.[7] Sharp had been engaged to nurse the Leakes'
child, which had contracted smallpox. During her time in their
employment, several items of domestic goods were alleged to have
gone missing, with the finger of suspicion pointing, variously, at

[5] See Peter King, *Crime and Law in England* op. cit. Chapter 1, pp. 44–6.
[6] *Tom Jones* op. cit. p. 84; see also Fielding's 'Essay on the Knowledge of the
Characters of Men' in *Miscellanies* (first published 1743) Vol 1. (Henry Knight
Miller (ed.) (Oxford: Clarendon Press 1972); see also Arlene Fish Wilner, 'Henry
Fielding and the Knowledge of Character' 18/1 *Modern Language Studies* (1988)
181–194.
[7] Old Bailey Sessions Papers t17421208–53.

Sharp and at the Leakes' maid. After a somewhat confusing testimonial narrative in which a welter of relevant circumstantial evidence is canvassed, the report settles into an extended, and colourful, analysis of the character of accused, prosecutrix and other witnesses:

'Mary Pritchet:
About six Months ago, Mrs Leake came to my House, and said she would swear a Robbery against this Woman and transport her; says this poor Woman, pray, Madam, do not expose me, your Maid gave them to me. Says she, you are a lying Bitch—She said she would either hang her or transport her.—I have trusted her in the Market, and never lost the Value of a Penny by her.

Sarah Sallery:
This Woman has been a Chair-woman a great many Times; I have trusted her with Linnen, Brass and Pewter, and other Things, which she might have stole; and I never lost any Thing, and I believe what she is charged with, is owing to their Maid; I believe her to be as honest a Creature as ever came into a House.

John Miltax:
I have known this Woman these two Years; I have trusted her with Linnen and other Things, and never lost any Thing in my Life.

Ann Crook:
She has worked at our Shop this Year and half; I have trusted her with Things and never missed any, and believe her to be a very honest Woman.

Joseph Calloway:
I have known her these two Years; she has carried Meat for me, and received the Money for it, and brought it me; I never found she wronged me, and believe her to be a very honest Woman.

Leake:
Mrs Pritchet and I have been at Law together, and she does it out of Spight.

Pritchet:
Yes, my Lord, we have been at Law together, and I believe the Prisoner at the Bar has a better Character than the Prosecutrix.
    Acquitted.'

Though Sarah Sharp's name would have been an excellent qualification for her appearance as a female thief in a mid-Eighteenth Century novel, in this lively contest for relative good character, her ability to draw on a solid record of employment is the key to her acquittal, as it is to a judgment in which Mrs Leake comes off distinctly the worse not withstanding her presumably higher social status. As a well established woman, Sharp was relatively fortunate among those accused of theft. As cases from the Old Bailey amply attest, character evidence from those ill equipped to establish their own standing was of limited or no avail, and the recital towards the end of many reports of a list of character testimonials, often unaccompanied by any reference to the status of the witness, often have a formulaic feel which is underlined by the terse conclusion of a guilty verdict and sentence. Here, for example, is the conclusion of the report of the trial of Mary Freeman,[8] also accused of theft in 1742:

'Abbot, Brunskell, Forsyth and Carter gave her the Character of an honest Woman. Guilty 10 d.; Whipping'.

In Freeman's case, however, it seems likely that the character evidence did at least secure her the benefit of a partial verdict: the assessment of the goods she was convicted of stealing at ten pence is almost certainly an under-valuation, and is hence a good example of Blackstone's argument that juries engaged in 'pious perjury' in finding means to save defendants from the death penalty.[9] The general application of capital punishment to thefts of a shilling or more made the securing of partial verdicts an important role of such evidence—as indeed in securing the jury's recommendation of the defendant to the court's mercy.[10] But to secure acquittal, particularly in the case of low status defendants in relation to whom the presumption of guilt would have operated with particular force, character evidence had to be persuasive indeed.

Both Sarah Sharp's case and Fielding's vignette encapsulate a number of themes which are important to our analysis. First and foremost, they epitomise the way in which networks of 'local knowledge' about reputation could be drawn upon by criminal justice decision-makers—notably Justices and jurors—in the mid-18th Century. Second, they suggest that evaluations of character were still focused, as in Judge's world of 'credit', on the external

---

[8] Old Bailey Sessions Papers t17421013–22.

[9] William Blackstone, *Commentaries on the Laws of England* Vol. IV (1765–9: University of Chicago Press 1979).

[10] See for example the case of Thomas Haven, Old Bailey Sessions Papers t17421208–47.

markers of role and status, albeit that, as in Sharp's case, social status is not conclusive where accumulated evidence of good reputation is strong. It is crucial to the meaning of Fielding's vignette that Adams is confirmed to be a clergyman, just as it is significant that Fielding carefully tells us that the source of verification is a 'squire'. It seems unlikely that this was merely exaggeration in the service of satire: in the informal process of lay justice which dominated the system, markers of status would have provided useful shorthands for assessments of credibility. Indeed Fielding was explicit about this in his non-fiction: in *An Enquiry in to the Causes of the Late Increase in Robbers* (1751), he argues that character evidence has 'great Weight' only when 'it comes from the Mouths of Persons, who have themselves some Reputation and Credit'.[11] And while, as demonstrated by Sharp's case, a formal trial might provide opportunities for a more elaborate assessment of individual credibility, the speed of hearings, at an average of twenty minutes, must itself have been far from inhospitable to such short-cuts. But whether individualised or standardised in their assessments of credibility, both vignette and real case share one central feature: their judgments, like that of the witness in Lying Joe's case quoted in Chapter I,[12] depend on an inference from external markers of character, in the sense of both role or type and reputation, to conduct. This is in striking contrast to the inverse inference from conduct to character, in the sense of disposition or intent, which is generally regarded as the predominant attributive mechanism in modern criminal law.

Equally significantly for our purposes, we should note one key difference between the literary and the legal trial. In Fielding's vignette Fanny, whose social position and gender both mark her out as of lower status, is not required to speak for herself. This is, of course, in contrast to the forthright articulacy of the female witnesses who dominate the debate about character in the report of Sarah Sharp's trial. So we might speculate that Fanny's passive silence is simply a product of Fielding's hierarchical view of the world. But, as I shall argue in more detail below, given that the criminal process was in the hands precisely of men like Fielding,

[11] Ed. Malvin R. Zirker (Oxford: Clarendon Press 1988) p. 163, quoted in Schramm, *Testimony and Advocacy in Victorian Law, Literature and Theology* p. 72.
[12] Old Bailey Sessions Papers t17451016-7.

this difference in attitude may itself have had an important bearing on the criminalisation of women.

Just as character evidence made frequent appearances in the criminal courts, in 18th Century novels as different as *Moll Flanders, Clarissa, Tom Jones* or *Cecilia*, references to character appear on virtually every other page, along with explicit or implicit ideas about the stability or fluidity of human character and about human beings' capacity to amend or 'work on' character. The centrality of 'character' in the 18th Century novels attests to the extraordinary importance of public reputation in a world which was at once relatively immobile and yet marked by emerging technologies of communication which allowed knowledge about character to travel—a combination epitomised by John Fielding's clever policy of using the press to publicise details about London suspects whose strangeness in the provinces might make them readily identifiable.[13] This echoes the way in which the 18th Century criminal process was able to draw, for the purposes of legitimation and practical co-ordination of judgment, on widely shared assumptions diffused across 18th Century society, as well as on networks of communication which made the resultant knowledge available to the criminal process. The centrality of reputation to 18th Century society is underlined in the novels by the use of striking metaphors either personifying character or rendering it as valuable property. In Smollett's *Expedition of Humphry Clinker*, one figure protests, 'don't go to murder my character', while another is described as 'bankrupt, both in means and reputation.'[14] And in *Tom Jones*, Fielding argues that 'to murder one's own reputation is a kind of suicide', and quotes from Othello:

'Who steals my purse steals trash; "tis something, nothing";
Twas mine, "tis his, and hath been slave to thousands;"
But he that filches from me my good name
Robs me of that WHICH NOT ENRICHES HIM
BUT MAKES ME POOR INDEED.'[15]

---

[13] Morgan and Rushton op. cit.
[14] *The Expedition of Humphry Clinker* op. cit. pp. 74, pp. 68–9; see also p. 103: 'As for the liberty of the press, like every other privilege, it must be restrained within certain bounds...If the lowest ruffian may stab your good-name with impunity in England, will you be so uncandid as to exclaim against Italy for the practice of common assassination? To what purpose is our property secured, if our moral character is left defenceless?'
[15] *Tom Jones* op. cit. pp. 201, 493.

Shifting conceptions of character

So both law and literature provide plentiful evidence of a persisting reliance on information about external markers of character in the process of attributing responsibility. But what, more precisely, is meant by 'character'? A number of more or less distinct inflections can be discerned, and these are of significance for our analysis. They move on two spectrums: from character as role, type or status at one end ('he thought a Schoolmaster the greatest Character in the world'[16] or 'a leading man in the House of Commons is a very important character'[17]) through to notions of character as individual reputation (as in the reference to Adams' 'very good Character' in the passage just cited: this reputational sense relates to a more specific sense of 'character' as reference or testimonial, as in 'dismissed without a character', but also refers to individually established credibility or respectability); and from character as moral quality or as evaluated disposition ('This Shyness... will recommend her Character to all our Female Readers...'[18]), through to character as individual psychological traits or personality ('her character was totally insipid'[19]). Often references move between these nuances, playing on the ambiguity: 'the ridicule I should meet with below upon a weakness so much out of my usual character'[20] (reputation shading into role or personality); 'the Character I was ambitious of attaining, was that of a fine Gentleman...'[21] (reputation allied to status, evoking the connotations of honour or virtue which derive from a particular social position). And, to paint with very broad brush strokes, in the novels we can discern two parallel shifts in terms of frequency and emphasis as we move from the earliest novels of Defoe, Richardson and Fielding to the novels of the late 18th and early 19th Century: from references to character as social status, type or public role to character as individually merited social reputation; and from disposition as moral character, in the Aristotelian sense of virtue or in the

---

[16] *Joseph Andrews* op. cit. p. 238.
[17] *Clarissa* (1747–8: Riverside Editions 1962) p. 248.
[18] *Joseph Andrews* op. cit. p. 166.
[19] Tobias Smollett, *The Expedition of Humphry Clinker* op. cit. p. 266.
[20] *Clarissa* op. cit. p. 265.
[21] *Joseph Andrews* op. cit. p. 214.

patriarchal sense of honour, to disposition as personality in the sense of psychological make-up.[22]

On the face of it, the pervasiveness of references to character cuts across Watt's distinction between a realism of representation and a realism of assessment considered in the last chapter. But on closer inspection, Watt's distinction allows us to discern another pattern, itself significant for the development of criminal justice. Whereas in the individualistic narratives of Defoe and Richardson, we can already see a concern with character in the sense of established reputation for good behaviour, along with an incipient concern with the psychological personality which becomes a primary focus of 19th Century realism, in Fielding's more patrician outlook, it is both disposition in the sense of moral character, and character in terms of established role—the place of characters, as it were, within a stratified society—which is more often evoked. And even in Richardson and Defoe, reputation is often established in relation to recognised social roles: while there may be—and, particularly in Defoe, often is—space for role play and the assumption of character, the roles or status positions in question are themselves well established: the honest merchant; the rake; the dutiful daughter and so on. Hence the two genres of literary realism reflect a process of transition from the world of credit to the world of credibility. In both forms of realism, however, the need to establish character in the sense of both moral and social status is recognised as an overwhelmingly important concern for social actors, while information about character given by external markers is seen as a significant resource in practices of judgment. Even in a world in

---

[22] Cf. Deidre Lynch's analysis of the pragmatic uses to which readers put understandings of character across the 18th Century in their attempts to make sense of their place in a changing social world: early meditations on how to represent character and to distinguish character from caricature; analyses of proper relations of sociability between characters in the 'novels of social circulation'; gradually giving way to analyses of depth of character and inner selfhood as mechanisms for both cultivating sympathy and establishing social distinctions in the novels of manners considered later in this chapter: *The Economy of Character* op. cit. The shifting emphasis which I sketch here should not be taken to imply that the idea of character as a valuable possession or form of social capital, or judgments of moral character, disappear from view: in fact they remain an important focus of novels, alongside explorations of psychology. For the importance—and variety of inflections—of 'character' in Victorian public discourse, see Stefan Collini, *Public Moralists: Political Thought and Intellectual Life in Britain 1850–1930* (Oxford University Press 1991) pp. 91–118.

which the interior is becoming important to ideas of responsibility, both individuals and legal institutions have to rely on external evidence. This is nicely reflected in the following exchange
between 'the female Quixote' and her rationalist interlocutor in
Charlotte Lennox's eponymous novel of 1752: 'Human Beings
cannot penetrate Intentions, nor regulate their Conduct but by
exterior Appearances...How is any oral, or written Testimony,
confuted or confirmed?' 'By comparing it,' says the Lady, 'with
the Testimony of others, or with the natural Effects and standing
Evidence of the Facts related, and sometimes by comparing it with
itself.'[23]

How does this argument relate to Wahrman's analysis of a
shift in regimes of identity? The Enlightenment world of early
English capitalism, in which empiricist psychology and social disembedding invited a new fluidity of human identity, undoubtedly produced the first person narratives of Defoe's *Moll Flanders*
or Richardson's *Pamela*, where the protagonists are, Wahrman
argues, not so much reporting on believable inner psychological states as performing roles for the reader. In this world, why
should the establishment of character nonetheless have depended
on articulation with recognised marks of social role, type or position? My suggestion is that, ironically, this possibility of role play
and mobility which growing individualism opened up accentuated rather than subverted the need to rely on external markers
produced by the status-oriented world which was slowly being
challenged. Only in the novels of the later 18th Century—notably
those of Frances Burney—do we begin to see the development
of ideas of moral character in which the realism of assessment is
becoming integrated with the realism of representation: in other
words, a confidence that evaluations of moral character and credibility can be genuinely trained on individuals rather than given
by status, whether 'natural' or assumed.[24] In the legal system,

[23] *The Female Quixote* op. cit. pp. 371, 377–8: note the striking similarity
between this injunction and several of the prudential maxims for assessing evidence already developing in 17th Century scientific discourse and discussed in
Chapter I: see Stephen Shapin, *A Social History of Truth* Chapter 5.
[24] And even in these novels, external markers of status remain important: see
for example Harriet Guest's persuasive reading of the way in which Burney's
Camilla's (op. cit.) social status affects shopkeepers' interpretation of her 'window-
shopping': *Small Change: Women, Learning, Patriotism, 1750–1810* (Chicago
University Press 2000) pp. 77–9.

where hierarchies of power implied by the property qualification for jurors relative to the average social status of defendants, absence of consistent legal representation, speed and non-technicality of hearing still pertained in Burney's time, the conditions for a genuine investigation of individual credibility were arguably yet longer in being constructed.

Whereas, in the 18th Century novels, issues about how human beings are to judge and evaluate each other are being investigated through the interplay of actors who are very firmly located within particular (received or assumed) social roles, and often characterised as particular types, as we move close to the 19th Century, the investigation—facilitated, of course, by the invention of the all-seeing third person narrator—is focused on the interior world of increasingly richly described human psychologies. To the 21st Century reader, the 18th Century novels read almost like restoration comedies: key figures have names which evoke their dispositions and social position: Squire Booby, Fanny Goodwill, Mr. Lovelace, Heartfree, Squire Allworthy, David Simple, Mrs Slipslop and so on. *Pace* Watt, these typecasting names are pervasive in the realism of representation even if they are more pronounced in the Augustan realism of assessment: to contemporaries, for example, the name Moll Flanders would instantly have signalled not only sexual promiscuity but also dishonesty.[25] Moll and her immediate descendants are vivid, and many of them, like Moll, are thoroughly rational agents: but they are not fully realised psychological individuals in the style of Austen, Brontë, Eliot or Hardy. No more, of course, were Dickens' suggestively named caricatures, or Walter Scott's schoolmaster Thwackers from *The Heart of Midlothian*, or most of the figures in *Vanity Fair* (with the gradual exception of the ultimately inaptly named Dobbin, whose depth of psychological development lifts the book from the status of a brilliant comedy of manners into a truly great realist novel). As Alex Woloch has shown, the continuation of a tradition of stereotyped minor characters is itself of interest for any socio-political reading of the novel: in an increasingly individualistic and democratised world, the novel's traditional focus on one or two central, 'round'

---

[25] 'Flanders', well known for prostitution, would have signalled Moll's sexual transgressions, while the evocation of valuable Flanders lace evokes her career as a thief: the sexual connotations of 'Moll' are evident: see Introduction to *Moll Flanders* op. cit. pp. 4, 7–9.

characters, surrounded by a panoply of typecast 'flat' characters, becomes increasingly uncomfortable, while the formal difficulties of accommodating a full array of individually painted, round characters within a manageable structure were, and remain, hard to resolve.[26] But the key point here is that in many 18th Century novels, even the central characters are, in the terms of this later characterisation, 'flat' rather than 'round': types rather than psychological individuals.

Overall, the novels' appeal to character is somewhat less prominent as we move into the 19th Century, is often focused on either individual moral character or personality and psychological disposition, and is less often concerned with social role or type. The reputational senses of character, however—including the technical sense of character as testimonial—remain important. This is significant when we consider that the centralising and systematising criminal justice reforms of the 19th Century developed slowly over many decades, and left intact a large degree of local autonomy which at least in certain rural areas continued to underpin significant regional variation and resort to informal justice.[27] This information about reputation may well have been gradually becoming less closely articulated with role or status, but some articulation persisted, and such information remained of central importance.[28]

From 'ancien' to modern regimes: honour, status and reputation

A vivid literary example of both the pervasive importance of reputation and the continuing role of status in establishing it throughout

[26] Alex Woloch, *The One and the Many* (Princeton University Press 2003); the distinction between 'round' and 'flat' characters is drawn from E.M. Forster's *Aspects of the Novel* op. cit.
[27] Carolyn A. Conley, *The Unwritten Law: Criminal Justice in Victorian Kent* op. cit.
[28] The importance of reputation to the conduct of social and economic life in 18th Century London is reflected in a distinctive institution of conflict resolution; the practice of publishing apologies in the press: see Donna T. Andrew, 'The press and public apologies in eighteenth-century London', in Norma Landau (ed.), *Law, Crime and English Society* op. cit. p. 208. Women featured far less prominently than men as both subjects and objects of these notices, though in Andrew's sample they make up a significantly larger proportion of recipients than of apologists (13% as opposed to 7.8%).

the 18th Century is William Godwin's *Caleb Williams*. Published in 1794, this book—originally entitled *Things As They Are*, evoking Godwin's politically motivated realism—presents a fascinating analysis of the persistence of the world of honour and status on the cusp of the 19th Century, as well as a searing indictment of almost every aspect of the late 18th Century criminal and penal process. Williams discovers that his apparently virtuous and widely respected master, Falkland, is guilty of a murder for which two other, lower status men were hanged. As a result of his ingenuous and, as it turns out, fatal curiosity, Williams manoeuvres Falkland into a private confession. To protect his honour and good name, Falkland ultimately revenges himself by having Williams falsely accused of theft and imprisoned in horrifyingly inhumane conditions. But in an excruciating twist to the plot, Falkland draws back from reliance on the formal legal process, and fails to appear at Williams' trial, leading to his release. He then employs someone to pursue Williams, relentlessly, from one end of the country to the other, with the specific design of preventing him from settling in any one place and establishing a reputation. And as Williams discovers, without reputation life as an individual is both materially and psychologically impossible.

In portraying Williams' inability to establish his veracity in testifying his innocence as against his high-status master, Godwin reminds us that the move away from a world in which power— including the power to command credit or credibility—was attendant on status was far from complete. Indeed, in the early part of the plot, when Falkland falls under suspicion of the murder and is called upon to defend himself before his brother Justices, he disdains even to rely on character evidence, asserting the independent status of his position: 'Great God: what sort of character is that which must be supported by witnesses?'[29] But the novel marks at many levels a world on the cusp between an economy of honour and character and one of formal law and reason. This is most clearly illustrated by the two very different endings which Godwin crafted. In the novel as published, Williams decides to return and confront

---

[29] *Caleb Williams* op. cit. p. 105. For further analysis of this novel's legal significance, see David Punter, 'Fictional Representation of Law in the 18th Century' 16 *Eighteenth–Century Studies* (1982) 47–74; Jan-Melissa Schramm, *Testimony and Advocacy in Victorian Law, Literature and Theology* op. cit. pp. 89–94; Elizabeth Judge, *Character Witnesses* op. cit. Chapter 7.

Falkland by making a formal accusation against him of the murder. At this stage Falkland capitulates, confesses his guilt, and, unable to survive the loss of his honour, dies three days later. This is, we might say, a thoroughly modern ending: the *ancien régime* dies with Falkland; law and reason triumph; and Godwin's portrayal of Williams' agonising guilt at having ultimately caused the loss of his former master's honour proceeds from a psychological humanism. The ending which Godwin originally contemplated, however, is rooted firmly in the *ancien régime*. In this version, Williams' accusation is defeated by Falkland, who appeals before the magistrates to his and Williams' respective characters: the credit attaching to his superior character is triumphant, and Williams' word, as someone of ill repute, and as a man who has questioned the veracity of his master, is of no worth.[30] The ambiguity between psychology and status is underlined by Williams' ultimate reflection; 'I set out to vindicate my character, but find I have no character to vindicate.'[31]

The moment of transition signified by the two endings of *Caleb Williams* was now coming to its end. A discernible shift away from the status economy of character was now well under way. But this did not imply the waning of importance of character as reputation, in either law or literature. This is nicely illustrated by *Vanity Fair*, published in 1847–8, but set in the earlier period of the Regency, and a book in which the ruthless, beautiful and talented Becky Sharp is set up as the foil to expose the shallowness of a world obsessed with marks of status and reputation yet in which it is in fact money and power which buy respect. Even in this relatively mobile world, however, Becky's bad reputation follows her around, even as far as the other side of the Channel, and underpins her exile from polite society.

Nor did the change in conceptual framework between the 18th and the 19th Century novels connote a complete rupture in terms of deeper concerns. References to character in the sense of public role may gradually decline, but the later novels, from Frances Burney on, are nonetheless exploring issues about character as disposition which already preoccupied their early 18th Century ancestors, and

---

[30] Op. cit. p. 341; this ending is rather more plausible than the one finally published, and includes a fascinating sketch of Williams' subsequent descent into madness.

[31] Op. cit. p. 337, from the ending as published.

which continue to perplex us today: free will and determinism, the role of environment and education, the fixity and stability (or otherwise) of human personality. Wahrman's *ancien régime* of fluidity and acceptable role play, however, is decisively over, and the orientation of the novel is firmly trained on the question of how to shape or perfect moral character, to recognise and evaluate moral character, and to manage wayward features of personal psychology.

So what do the novels tell us about the broad conditions which underpinned the gradual move from *ancien* towards modern regimes, and from character as type, assumed role, honour or virtue to character as individual reputation or psychology? Significant here is the way in which the 18th Century novels exhibit prevailing social anxieties, particularly about the possible de-civilising and de-moralising impact of commerce, of urbanisation and of increasing social mobility in the emerging individualistic world.[32] The theme of the danger and corrupting influence of town life, and of London and the spa towns in particular, and of access to too much readily disposable wealth, is a constant from *Clarissa* through *Joseph Andrews* and *Tom Jones*, to the ultimate status of London as the pinnacle of *Vanity Fair*. In Frances Burney's *Cecilia*[33] and Maria Edgeworth's *Belinda*, London is the fount of self-interest, evil, temptation, deracination from a life of quiet connection and decency, while Mr. Matthew Bramble in Tobias Smollett's *Humphrey Clinker* constantly returns in his letters to the enjoyable practice of drawing an unfavourable comparison, in terms of civility and hygiene, between London and the country.[34]

Already in this book, published in 1771, we are witnessing an awareness of, and anxiety about, the breakdown of the conditions of existence of what had for long been a very stable basis of both

---

[32] For a fascinating account of the ways in which anxieties about the impact of commerce realised themselves in shifting images of child murder in law, literature and painting, see Josephine McDonagh, *Child Murder and British Culture 1720–1900* (Cambridge University Press 2003) Chapter 1.

[33] (1782: Oxford World's Classics 1999); on the corruption of London, see also Henry Mackenzie, *The Man of Feeling* (1771: op. cit.); Sarah Fielding, *The Adventures of David Simple, Containing An Account of his Travels Through the Cities of London and Westminster, In the Search of A Real Friend* (1744: op. cit.).

[34] On anxieties about crime and disorder in London from the late 17th Century, see J.M. Beattie, *Policing and Punishment in London* op. cit., and see further below pp. 91ff.

legitimation and practical co-ordination in the criminal process and indeed in the social order more generally: relative value consensus, stable power relations between social groups and readily available information about reputation key among them. Each of these conditions of social ordering and—of almost equal importance—faith in their vigour, were undoubtedly eroded by urbanisation (with the population of London growing from 575,000 in 1700 to 675,000 in 1750 and to 900,000 by the end of the Century[35]), by greater social mobility attendant on the growth of trade, and by the development of a capitalist economy. As we shall see, these anxieties were to have important implications for the criminalisation of women.

Of particular significance here was the emergence of a bourgeois and merchant class (the primary audience for the emerging genre of the novel)[36] whose interests and values differed significantly from those of the landed elites, and of an urban working class untied from the rural social structures and quasi-feudal institutions which had proved such an effective source of informal governance (and which continued as such in rural areas well into the 19th Century[37]). Gradually, the criminal process responded by beginning to develop ideas of responsibility which were relatively independent of the content of the norms breached; which could be proven—once the relevant institutions were put in place—in the trial forum; and which could be controlled by professionals rather than by a jury. Lay judgments of 'manifest criminality' rooted in local knowledge and common sense, in other words, began to be tempered by an increasingly elaborate set of exclusionary rules of evidence and by the 'lawyerisation' of the trial.[38] But this development took many decades to accomplish, just as the construction of a code of public morality adequate to disciplining the forces unleashed by capitalist culture has been a long time in the making (if indeed it has yet been accomplished). Part of the cultural perplexity which animates *Moll Flanders* is, as Juliet Mitchell put

---

[35] Allyson N. May, *The Bar and the Old Bailey 1750–1850* op. cit. pp. 8–9.

[36] See Ian Watt, *The Rise of the Novel* op. cit.: in criminal justice as in politics, the ideas and values of this emerging bourgeoisie struggled for well over a century for institutional realisation.

[37] Carolyn A. Conley, *The Unwritten Law* op. cit.

[38] On the importance of the increasing professional control of the criminal trial, see John Langbein, *The Origins of Adversary Criminal Trial* op. cit; and Jan-Melissa Schramm, *Testimony and Advocacy in Victorian Law, Literature and Theology* op. cit. Chapter 1, especially p. 55ff.

it, 'a question of the similarity of the crimes and the laws against them, of "acceptable society" and its "underside".[39] We now need to turn to the story of how this gradual shift in both criminal justice and informal moral code came about, and of its implications for women.

Sensibility in the Service of Capitalism: From Moll to Clarissa *via* Pamela

The character of feminine virtue

There is plenty of evidence, then, in the 18th Century novels about the place of character and reputation in the attribution of responsibility during that period. But, in the light of Feeley's and Little's argument about 'the vanishing female', we now need to consider the ways in which judgments of good and bad character were gendered. If criminal responsibility-attribution was shifting slowly from the 18th Century through the 19th Century from a character-based to a capacity-based pattern, this might help to explain the gradual decline in women's recorded involvement in crime. In the 18th Century, judgments of good and bad character would of course have been gendered. But they might nonetheless have been susceptible of mobilisation as much for women as for men: what counted as good and bad character for men and women might be different, but each might suffice to underpin an attribution of criminal responsibility.[40] Indeed, there might even be reason to think that assumptions of bad character were particularly readily available in relation to women. Moll Flanders, for example, rails against the unfairness that it was normal for men to inquire into a woman's character and reputation but unseemly for a woman to do

[39] Juliet Mitchell, 'Moll Flanders, The Rise of Capitalist Woman' op. cit. p. 204.
[40] This would have amounted, as Garthine Walker has put it in relation to the 17th Century, to a situation of incommensurable rather than unequal principles of judgment: *Crime, Gender and Social Order* op. cit. Chapters 1, 5 (on property offences) and 7; see in particular the argument about incommensurability on p. 158.

the same in relation to a man; she also notes the power of gossips to ruin male as well as female reputation (with typical resourcefulness, Moll exploits this circulation of reputation by manipulating it, propagating false information about her fortune to entrap her Lancashire husband).[41]

But if in the latter part of the century the association of criminal responsibility with proof of agency and capacity was growing stronger, this might have prompted a shift in gender patterns of responsibility-attribution. For the faculties of reason and self control in terms of which Enlightenment philosophy understood responsibility were themselves increasingly believed to be more liberally (as it were) bestowed upon men—as Mary Wollstonecraft noted in her coruscating attack on Rousseau's view that 'woman is naturally weaker than man' and that she is justly denied 'the rights of reason'.[42] The long-standing association of reason and intellect with masculinity, and of emotionality and the body with femininity, was arguably becoming reinforced by two further cultural developments. The first was the emergence of a highly gendered culture of sensibility—another object of Mary Wollstonecraft's critical analysis—in which women came to bear primary responsibility for embodying and propagating the marks of respectability which distinguish the emerging bourgeois class.[43] This is exemplified by heroines like *Clarissa*, *Cecilia* and Fanny Price, while it is mercilessly satirised in Thackeray's

[41] *Moll Flanders* op. cit. pp. 113–14; 115ff.
[42] *A Vindication of the Rights of Woman* (1792: Penguin Classics 1985) pp. 55, 242. It is important, of course, not to overstate the extent to which the late 17th and early 18th Century saw a real, if temporary, change in perceptions of women. After all, many Augustan authors expressed pervasive skepticism about women's autonomy, as well as engaging in vituperative expressions of rank misogyny, notably in the form of two famous satirical poems—Alexander Pope's multi-volume *Dunciad* (1728–43: London: Longman 1999) and Jonathan Swift's *Corinna* (1731) in which Eliza Haywood, the actress, playwright, creator and editor of *The Female Spectator* from 1744–46, and successful author of amatory fiction (see for example *Love in Excess: Or, the Fatal Enquiry*, 1719–20: Broadview Literary Texts 2000), is a notable target. On the Augustans' attitude to women, see Carolyn A. Williams, 'Another Self in the Case: Gender, Marriage and the Individual in Augustan Literature' op. cit. p. 97 at pp. 102–3. See also Janet Todd, *Sensibility: An Introduction* (London: Methuen 1987).
[43] Ibid. On the establishment from the late 17th Century of Societies for the Reformation of Manners, see J.M. Beattie *Crime and the Courts in England* op. cit. pp. 621–4, and *Policing and Punishment in London* op. cit. pp. 54, 58, 61, 66, 237–8.

shallow Amelia of *Vanity Fair*, whose sensibility is such that she can burst into tears at the mere thought of someone's suffering, yet who is incapable of understanding real love. The second was the gradual construction of an ideology which explicitly circumscribed not merely the modes of comportment within which women's activity and agency could be exercised but also the proper terrain over which they could be exercised.[44] How, and why, did these developments come about?

In trying to answer these questions, the transition from Defoe's *Moll Flanders* in 1722 to Richardson's *Clarissa* in 1747 is of particular interest, as is the birth of a heroine who arguably marked a key staging post in the journey from the transgressive to the disciplined heroine: Richardson's *Pamela*, who made her appearance in 1740. The idea with which Juliet Mitchell framed her analysis of Moll—the 'capitalist woman'—would apply readily to *Pamela*: a poor servant girl who uses not only her virtue but also her intelligence, enterprise, courage, cunning (and, it must be admitted, looks) to attain her reward. Resisting the attempts at seduction of her wealthy master, Mr. B., Pamela survives a period of imprisonment and a panoply of forms of physical and psychological coercion, finally persuading him to marry her. The radical vision of a woman able to choose her partner and to do so on the basis of affection both underpinned the novel's popularity with women and presaged a real social change.[45] Not so the strength and enterprise through which this end is achieved: capitalist woman of the genre of Moll and Pamela seems to have been stifled in her infancy—or at least administered a sedative which kept her docile (or, like Becky Sharp, exiled from respectability) for a couple of centuries.

In Richardson's work, the change came very quickly. If we look at his next novel, *Clarissa*, we see a different picture.[46] Under the influence, perhaps, of Fielding's pungent critique of *Pamela* as a

---

[44] See Lucia Zedner, *Women, Crime and Custody in Victorian England* (Oxford University Press 1991) Chapter 1.

[45] See Watt, *The Rise of the Novel* Chapter V; the impact of developing family structures is discussed in the next section of this chapter.

[46] As McKeon observes, there is a real sense in which Pamela is a progressive heroine, while Clarissa is a conservative one: *The Origins of the English Novel* op. cit. pp. 380, 418.

hypocrite whose behaviour tended to subvert the social order by encouraging servants to seduce their masters in the hope of marriage, Richardson's second heroine is decisively punished for her wilful moment of intuitive self-assertion. Personally favoured and talented—and from a more privileged social background than Pamela—Clarissa resists her family's financially motivated attempts to marry her to a man she despises, and questions their distrust of the attractive but rakish Lovelace, the supposed suitor of her sister. Lovelace rewards Clarissa's trust by abducting, imprisoning and, finally, drugging and raping her. Clarissa ultimately manages to escape, and then—significantly—as it were punishes herself by refusing to invoke the law to indict Lovelace and by subsiding gradually into a pious death.[47] Fielding, I am sorry to have to report, applauded, showering *Clarissa* with a degree of approbation proportionate to the opprobrium which he had heaped on her elder sister.

Clarissa, significantly, is doomed the minute she leaves the protection of the family; her actual virtue cannot in normal social space survive the conventional ruin of her character, itself invited by her flight—however provoked—from the patriarchal scene of order. But there is modern individualism here too, and not solely in Clarissa's indomitable will. For the more amiable characters—the formally mute but entirely eloquent voice of the novelist among them—recognise her virtue as triumphing over social forms; and it is this individual virtue which is upheld, within Richardson's religious message, as the object of our admiration and as, ultimately, triumphant. But that virtue is premised on the most rigorous standards of religious devotion and moral comportment. Between the worlds of *Pamela* and of *Clarissa*, the idea moreover emerges that resort to law is in some sense a violation of the norms of feminine sensibility and religious duty. This is a claim made explicitly by Clarissa, and one which is clearly independent of any assessment of her likelihood of prevailing in a prosecution for rape (albeit that

[47] There has been considerable debate about this aspect of the novel, and my interpretation is clearly not the only way of looking at the issue. Schramm, for example, points out that in refusing resort to law, Richardson preserves the centrality of his sympathetic viewpoint, which is reflected in Clarissa's first person account, unmediated by the interference of a male-dominated legal reading: *Testimony and Advocacy in Victorian Law, Literature and Theology* op. cit. p. 11.

she would have understood her chances of legal success to be compromised by the appearance of her collusion in her own abduction). And this idea that it is somehow inappropriate to the norms of polite feminine comportment to resort to law contains the seeds of a privatisation of, as Mary Wollstonecraft put it in her one (unfinished) novel, 'the wrongs of woman'.[48] This was, significantly, in contrast to the emerging early modern evidence of women's relatively active use of the legal system through mechanisms such as defamation cases, echoed by both Moll's strategic use of law and the litigation between Mrs Leake and Mrs Pritchet mentioned in the report of Sarah Sharp's trial.[49]

What are we to make of this dramatic transition from *Moll* to *Pamela* and then to *Clarissa*? Combining an insistent moral message about the rewards of virtue with a titillating account of Pamela's constant danger, Richardson created, as Watt memorably put it, 'a work that could be praised from the pulpit and yet attacked as pornography, a work that gratified the reading public with the combined attractions of a sermon and a striptease.'[50] The work was read—and was meant to be read—as a moral example; its sub-title, after all, was *Virtue Rewarded*. Alexander Pope accordingly complimented Richardson, *via* the physician George Cheney, that 'he had read Pamela with great approbation and pleasure, and wanted a Night's Rest in finishing it, and says it will do more good than a great many of the new Sermons'.[51] And yet it was equally taken up as a model for pornographic writing—

---

[48] *Maria, or The Wrongs of Woman* (1798: Mineola, New York: Dover Publications 2005).

[49] See Kermode and Walker (eds.), *Women, Crime and the Courts* op. cit.; Walker, *Crime, Gender and Social Order* op. cit. Chapter 6. Carolyn Conley notes that in Kent, over a century after the publication of *Clarissa*, the idea of being at once a rape complainant and a respectable woman is an oxymoron: the very fact of bringing her sexuality into the public sphere defines a woman as outside respectability (*The Unwritten Law* op. cit. pp. 83–5). The observation is interesting in the light of the public reaction to *Tess of the d'Urbervilles* (see above, pp. 4–5, note 10). Beyond sexual cases, as some of the testimony in Sarah Sharp's case quoted above shows, women remained in the 18th Century willing to threaten and use defamation law to protect their reputations—another piece of evidence of their own sense of the importance of maintaining good character: see further Robert Shoemaker, *Gender in English Society 1660–1850: The emergence of separate spheres* (London: Longman 1998) Chapter 7.

[50] *The Rise of the Novel* op. cit. p. 173.

[51] Keymer and Sabor, *Pamela in the Marketplace* op. cit. p. 25.

notably in John Cleland's *Memoirs of a Woman of Pleasure* (1749).[52] In this ambiguity lay the seeds of a heated controversy about the book. It is easy to imagine that the thin-skinned Richardson would have been stung by Fielding's merciless, and hilarious, take-off, *Shamela*,[53] which has the eponymous heroine declaring in a letter to her mother that she 'had thought once of making a little fortune by my person', but now intends 'to make a great one by my virtue…,' and in which Mr. B. is recast as 'Squire Booby'.[54] But Fielding was not the only contemporary to find fault with *Pamela*, and her mixed public reception affords a fascinating window onto early 18th Century assumptions about both class and gender.

On the one hand, *Pamela* had an extraordinary commercial success and cultural impact. The book reached a wide and socially diverse audience. Though reliable figures on how many copies were sold are not available, we have some indicative information: the book had appeared in no fewer than five editions by the end of 1741;[55] the third edition of 1741—only a year after the book's appearance—was printed in a run of 3,000 copies; and it is thought that about 20,000 copies of authorised editions were printed and sold by the end of that year.[56] Combining these and other facts with what is known about the contemporary reading public, it has been estimated that *Pamela* may have had as many as 180,000 readers by the end of the 18th Century.[57] Moreover the book spawned an industry of artefacts such as prints, waxworks, paintings, ornaments, poems, theatrical productions, unauthorised versions, satires and polemics. The commercial exploitation of *Pamela*'s success was open to anyone and, as Keymer and Sabor

[52] Better known as *Fanny Hill* (1749: Ware: Wordsworth Classics 2000); on Cleland's deployment of patterns and tropes from both *Pamela* and *Shamela*, see Keymer and Sabor, *Pamela in the Marketplace* op. cit. pp. 104–7.

[53] *An Apology for the Life of Mrs Shamela Andrews* (1741: Penguin Classics 1999). Readers may recall that we encountered a member of the Booby family in Fielding's account of Rev. Adams' arrest quoted earlier in this chapter: *Joseph Andrews* (op. cit.) in fact continued the satire on *Pamela* by casting its eponymous hero as her supposed brother. As McKeon has observed, the book is formally a rewrite of *Pamela* with the genders reversed: *The Origins of the English Novel* op. cit. p. 399.

[54] *Shamela* op. cit. p. 95.

[55] Margot C. Finn, *The Character of Credit* op. cit. p. 26.

[56] Thomas Keymer and Peter Sabor, *Pamela in the Marketplace* op. cit. pp. 5, 20.

[57] Naomi Tadmor, *Family and Friends in Eighteenth-Century England* op. cit. p. 15, n. 42.

put it, 'though Richardson had all the protectionist instincts of a one-man Disney Corporation, he had none of the legal arsenal'.[58]

The 'Pamela industry'—possibly including some of the more vituperative attacks—may therefore have been encouraged by Richardson, in a demonstration of entrepreneurial *savoir faire* geared to maximising sales in a world which still had no developed institution of intellectual property. But it also reflected growing literacy among middling people and in particular among female domestic servants, who found this tale of female assertion and cunning, and of social mobility, highly appealing. This was a world in which the over-representation of women in the population presented real barriers to marriage, while the demeaning attitude to spinsterhood made single life an unattractive prospect. Furthermore the low wages for many men and women made men reluctant to marry unless a woman brought a dowry. Yet marriage was the only escape for domestic servants from a life of virtual slavery.[59] In this context, the vision of an upwardly mobile marriage based on affection would have presented a delicious prospect to many women readers. On the other hand, patricians like Fielding regarded Pamela's feminine delicacy (represented in a remarkable capacity to faint or weep at opportune moments) as inauthentic, saw her frequent protestations of virtue as a mark of hypocrisy,[60] and decried her triumphant history as subversive of social order.

[58] See Keymer and Sabor, *Pamela in the Marketplace* op. cit. p. 52. They argue that there is persuasive evidence that Richardson went so far as to encourage, perhaps even organise, some of the more hostile attacks on *Pamela* as a way of maintaining public interest in the original (see pp. 34–6). In their view, Fielding's critique was aimed primarily at Richardson's exaggerated practices of promotion and, in particular, of soliciting 'puffs', and at the book's narrow conception of virtue as chastity, rather than at its socially subversive implications: see in particular pp. 6–7; 31.

[59] On the 'crisis of marriage' in the early 18th Century, see Watt, *The Rise of the Novel* op. cit. Chapter V.

[60] As Watt notes (ibid), these criticisms of *Pamela* are not unrelated to the novel's epistolary form, in which Pamela herself is the almost exclusive witness, giving the reader access to alternative evaluations of her conduct only through her own reports of other's behaviour. On the 'Pamela controversy', see also Elizabeth Judge, *Character Witnesses* op. cit. Chapter 5.

The civilising character of women: from Clarissa to the conduct manual

In rewarding Pamela's 'virtue' in the sense of her defence of her own chastity, Richardson was also rewarding a level of financially oriented strategy of which Moll would definitely have been proud. But Pamela's success, unlike Moll's, depended on an exaggerated (and hence perhaps incredible) cultivation of norms of femininity: an exquisite sense of the polite limits not only on sexual intimacy but also on cross-class relationships, reflected in particular in the nice distinctions which Pamela draws throughout the novel between gifts and favours which she should and should not accept. Why should female strategy and self-assertion have been troubling in a world already turning to capitalism? The answer seems to be that the world of status was far from extinct, and that in the wake of greater class mobility, new forms of distinction geared to the establishment and recognition of social status and credibility began to be constructed. As Margot Finn perceptively puts it, 'Richardson's novel offers not a narrative of the triumph of possessive individualism, but rather a case study in the partial transition from gift to commodity, from status to contract, in modern England. In *Pamela*, the tension and interplay between gift and commodity exchange are key moral markers of relations between character, providing a symbolic shorthand by which Richardson signals the value he ascribes to the choices made by individual agents in the economic and social sphere.'[61]

For both men and women, cultivated manners and particular modes of dress—like the emerging notion of a distinction between high and low culture[62]—were key to this new signalling system. And in the emerging code of manners, gender mobility, having opened up for a few decades, was being yet more strictly controlled, with ideas of fixed sexual difference reasserting themselves. As Sylvana Tomaselli puts it, 'Although by no means the only image the eighteenth century had of itself, the

---

[61] Margot C. Finn, *The Character of Credit* op. cit. p. 32: for Finn's overall reading of the novel's significance in expressing the dilemmas of gender and class in early capitalism, see pp. 26–34.
[62] See Lynch, *The Economy of Character* op. cit. Part Two.

most distinctive self-perception was of a society embarking on a profound change in manners. Women featured prominently in many of these self-portrayals of the age. They did so and were seen to do so as more than mere adornments to the new salon culture. They entertained, read, wrote, translated, conducted experiments, travelled, and reported on their travels. More than the accumulated sum of the achievements of individual women, the sex as a whole was thought to have instigated and kindled the civilising process.'[63]

The closing down of the transgressive gender performances of the late 17th and early 18th Centuries, in other words, appears to have been a function of the need to resolve some key tensions produced by a newly mobile social order amid the spread of urban capitalism—tensions about how to live, and about how to make judgments, which surface early in the political and philosophical writings of the Enlightenment. Contemporary analysis diverged markedly across this terrain. On the one hand, thinkers like physician and satirist Bernard Mandeville welcomed unambiguously the logic of individualism, pleasure, growth and consumption which was implied by the emerging capitalist economy: significantly, he also denied the assertion of natural sex difference and applauded sexual expression by both men and women. Like David Hume, Mandeville's view was that the expression of even selfish individual preferences would lead to social benefits overall: hence the subtitle of his famous tract, *The Fable of the Bees* (1723), was *Private Vices, Publick Benefits*. Others, however, worried about what would be lost in the move to a contractual economy, and some of them—a notable example being the Earl of Shaftesbury—argued for a replacement of the old status society by a more liberal society tempered or disciplined by a 'culture of politeness' or taste.[64]

---

[63] 'The Death and Rebirth of Character in the Eighteenth Century', in Roy Porter (ed.), *Rewriting the Self* op. cit. p. 84 at pp. 86–7; for the classic statement of the emergence of modern manners, see Norbert Elias, *The Civilising Process* (Volumes 1–3) (1939: New York: Pantheon 1978, 1982 and 1983 respectively).

[64] At a philosophical level, this is of course a debate which continues to reverberate in moral and political theory, with Bentham's robust assertion of the moral equivalence of pushpin and poetry a powerful metaphor for the Mandevillean perspective. On Mandeville, Shaftesbury and Smith, see further G.J. Barker-Benfield, *The Culture of Sensibility* op. cit.; E.J. Hundert, 'The European Enlightenment and the History of the Self' in Roy Porter (ed.), *Rewriting the Self* op. cit. p. 72.

The currency of philosophical ideas—notably Locke's psychology of sensual susceptibility to received impressions, and Hume's epistemology—also had an impact. Combining as they did with the new fluidity of socio-economic relations in the cities, their implication of an instability of personal identity was at once liberating and unsettling to the notion of unified selfhood. And the unsettled feelings fed the powerful preoccupation with codes of norms—of manners, civility and education—which promised both to tame the unbridled forces of capitalism and individualism and to re-stabilise people's sense of who they were. In this context, norms of taste were as important as explicitly moral norms: indeed, taste became a form of morality. Furthermore, the new culture of sensibility and politeness promised a solution to a problem which both preoccupied individuals and posed difficulties for institutional mechanisms of social judgment: that of how to evaluate or assess individual character. It did so by developing a refined set of mechanisms for signalling reliability or credibility independently of received status—as was necessary in the context of the emergence of a new class of social and economic interests, and as was indispensable to the interpretive abilities of jurors and other social actors.[65]

But how was the emerging code of manners constructed and propagated? The burgeoning press, of course, played a key role, through a wide variety of literary forms. This is nicely illustrated by a perusal of the boudoir reading of some heroines of the period. For example, in 1801, Maria Edgeworth's *Belinda*'s[66] literary diet juxtaposed Adam Smith, whose influential *Theory of Moral Sentiments*[67] sought to tread a middle path between the extremes of unbridled egoism and status conservatism, with another important resource in the development of refined sensibility in the service of

---

[65] This is not to say that a distinctive 'middle class' emerged at this stage: see Dror Wahrman, *Imagining the Middle Class* (Cambridge University Press 1995).

[66] (1801: Oxford World's Classics 1994). Note that Edgeworth, like many of her 18th Century literary peers including Eliza Haywood and Samuel Richardson, was the author of not only novels but also conduct manuals and treatises on education: see for example *Letters for Literary Ladies, to which is added, An Essay on the noble science of self-justification* (1795: London: Everyman 1993), discussed in Harriet Guest, *Small Change* op. cit. pp. 315–319; on Haywood and Richardson, see Naomi Tadmor, *Family and Friends in Eighteenth-Century England* op. cit. Chapters 2, 3 and 7.

[67] *The Theory of Moral Sentiments* (1759: New York: Cosimo 2007).

capitalism: the conduct manual or sermon. While James Fordyce's *Sermons to Young Women* (1765) was undoubtedly the most popular of these,[68] and the most pervasive in novels, the genre as a whole flourished. And much of it was specifically directed to (as well as written by) women—a notable example being Susanna Maria Cooper's *The Exceptional Mother* (1769). The conduct manual exemplifies the intimate link between aesthetic and moral norms at this period. Robert Shoemaker has estimated that about 500 such books were published between 1693 and 1760.[69] Thus the didacticism of novels—sometimes argued to have constituted a secular version of Methodism, the religion most closely trained on individual emotional experience[70]—was reinforced by, and fed into, a burgeoning genre of other literary products to which novelists themselves contributed, in a move itself underpinned by the developing technology of the press during the 18th Century. Among these we should not forget the highly didactic, and equally influential, Augustan voices of Addison and Steele in the *Spectator* and the *Tatler*—nor that of Eliza Haywood's parallel *Female Spectator*.

Since novels were written both for and, in many cases, by representatives of the new economic interests, it is hardly surprising that they are in themselves a rich source of insight into the culture of sensibility and its implications for women. What is perhaps more surprising is that the patrician world view, and with it the status-based economy of character, persisted alongside a more egalitarian individualism in the genre. But it was a new economy of status, and responsibility for expressing and propagating it was moreover increasingly consigned to women. Certainly, feeling became a valued attribute for men, too, and the acceptability of physical violence was declining across the board. This had, among other things, decisive implications for the social acceptability of practices such as duels,[71] which were rooted in the old status-based economy of honourable character favoured by *Caleb Williams'* Mr. Falkland. But it was women's—or, rather, wives' and daughters'—cultivation

---

[68] And the exemplar favoured by Belinda: James Fordyce *Sermons to Young Women* (1765: London: Cadell 1809): as we shall see in Chapter III, Fordyce was still being read by literary women well into the 19th Century.
[69] *Gender in English Society 1660–1850* op. cit.
[70] J. Paul Hunter, *Before Novels* op. cit. Chapter 10.
[71] See Stephen Shapin, *A Social History of Truth* op. cit. pp. 107–14.

of politeness and taste which was becoming both the marker of men's social status and a driver of consumption. Already in *Pamela*, the last 18th Century literary representative of mobile capitalist woman, the markers of exaggerated feminine politeness, which became crucial to the embodied credibility of women, are present, even if in somewhat suspect form: Pamela constantly asserts the authenticity of both her feelings and her narrative of virtue by invoking signals such as blushing, weeping or fainting which, as Fielding sceptically noted, conveniently also often serve to advance her strategy.

Clarissa, equally imbued with feminine sensibility, but to very much less instrumental effect, seems, with hindsight, to have been a turning point: her virtues rewarded only in the next world, and her rather innocent transgression of social order sealing her fate in this one. From the mid-18th Century on, what it means to be a female heroine in the genre of literary realism is tied up with self-denial and the containment of self-expression. The odd bright spark appears, even from the pen of Henry Fielding: Sophia Western, the spirited admirer of *Tom Jones*, defies her father and risks her social position to pursue Tom, for example. But her transgression of male authority is contained firmly within a conventional narrative which leads inexorably to marriage, and indeed to a marriage which turns out to be socially appropriate within a status economy of birth, even though none of the parties is aware of it at the outset. And increasingly, equally importantly from the point of view of emerging ideas of social order, women are asked to pull off the trick of exhibiting exquisite sensibility while exercising adequate self-control. Thus in the novel of social circulation, Frances Burney's *Evelina* (1778) and *Camilla* (1796) are sent out into the world equipped with brains, beauty and sensibility, but they are tutored by social, economic and emotional experiences which teach them, in effect, the importance of inhibiting self-expression. In Fanny Price we have perhaps the supreme representation of this culture of exquisite yet controlled female sensibility: she spends most of the course of *Mansfield Park* (1814) engaged in a tremendous struggle to contain her feelings, sustain her values and comport herself with dignity in very hostile circumstances.

Hard as it may be for us as early 21st Century readers to appreciate that there could have been anything radical in this normative image, it is important to note that Burney's, Edgeworth's and Austen's case for self-mastery had some significant affinities with Wollstonecraft's rationalist feminism.[72] Certainly, there were important differences: Wollstonecraft for example took a far more radical position on women's right to express their feelings. In this respect, she and her contemporary and admirer Mary Hays[73] stand in striking contrast to the idealisation of self-control to be found in Austen, Burney and Edgeworth. Yet though they celebrate exquisite self-containment and politely avert their gaze from the exploitative power of men to which Wollstonecraft drew attention, they shared with her a view of women, when properly educated, as just as capable as men intellectually, though all too often distorted by an excessive sentimentality invited by Romance and by the less tutored versions of the cult of sensibility. In the context of a generalised cultural and legal tendency to view women as less capable than men of self-mastery (the gender of the term is hardly accidental),[74] this was indeed a radical thought. Fanny is often seen as Jane Austen's least interesting heroine: passive, weak, pallid. It is crucial to my argument that this is a very basic misunderstanding. In fact, Austen would have seen Fanny as an image of strength and of individual responsibility—moreover of strength and responsibility in a specifically feminine genre: Fanny's[75] is a moral strength, exercised in private and, often, in silence. That the ideal of sensibility as developed towards the end of the 18th Century came to be associated with a high degree of not only emotional sensitivity but also self-control suggests a basis for rebuttal of the idea that the feminine was unambiguously associated with weakness.[76] And

[72] As Harriet Guest rightly points out, these writers also share with Wollstonecraft a distinctively modern notion of interior selfhood and personal authenticity (itself distinctive of Wahrman's 'modern regime of identity'): *Small Change* op. cit. p. 292.

[73] *Memoirs of Emma Courtney* (1796: Oxford World's Classics 1996).

[74] See Dana Rabin, *Identity, Crime and Legal Responsibility* op. cit. Chapter 4.

[75] Like Anne Elliot's in *Persuasion* (1818: Penguin Classics 1998).

[76] See Dana Rabin, *Identity, Crime and Legal Responsibility* op. cit. Chapter 4. For Jane Austen's own critique of an excessive sensibility untutored by self-control, see *Sense and Sensibility* (1811: Penguin Classics 1995), in which one sister's volatile emotionality is contrasted with another's quiet good sense. And notwithstanding the fact that its romanticism and lack of realism were satirised by Austen and other female writers of her ilk, the same critique of excessive sensibility and celebration of reason is to be found in key examples of the Gothic genre: see Ann Radcliffe, *The Mysteries of Udolpho* (1792: Penguin Classics 1998) pp. 5, 21, 281. Even Charlotte Dacre's *Zofloya or The Moor* (1806: Oxford World

here, notwithstanding the gendered noun, women were expected to conform perhaps to a greater degree than—though in a different way from—men.

Women, Marriage and Legal Subjecthood: From *Roxana* to *Cecilia*

In this context, the first half of the 18th Century can be seen as a fascinating set of cross-cutting strains. On the one hand, we have the liberating and disembedding forces of the *ancien régime* of identity and of early capitalism, bringing with them the promise of an entirely different set of gender arrangements. On the other, we have the need to stabilise and co-ordinate meaning and communication in a newly individualistic world—a need whose fulfillment involved a substantial borrowing from older repertoires of status as well as the creation of new norms of conduct. As we saw in relation to the reception of *Pamela*, one particular site of cultural perplexity was marriage—an institution whose highly gendered legal form was not settled until the middle of the 18th Century.[77] It has been argued—most influentially by Lawrence Stone—that the nuclear family was now beginning to take a more central place in English society.[78] The idea of companionate marriage based on

Classics 1997), an extreme instance of the Gothic genre which has its thoroughly nasty heroine fall into the clutches of the devil, emphasises the role of upbringing in shaping her inability to curb her own desires.

[77] The laws on marriage and divorce also attracted Wollstonecraft's critical analysis: see *A Vindication of the Rights of Woman* op. cit. Chapter IV.

[78] On the development of ideas and structures of family and kinship during this period, see Lawrence Stone, *The Family, Sex and Marriage in England, 1500–1800* (London: Weidenfeld and Nicolson 1977) and *Broken Lives: Separation and Divorce in England 1660–1857* (Oxford University Press 1993); Randolph Trumbach, *The Rise of the Egalitarian Family: Aristocratic Kinship and Domestic Relations in Eighteenth-Century England* (New York 1978); Robert Shoemaker, *Gender in English Society 1660–1850: The emergence of separate spheres?* op. cit. Chapter 4; Ruth Perry, *Novel Relations: The Transformations of Kinship in English Literature and Culture 1748–1818* (Cambridge University Press 2004). The debate about Stone's assertion that the nuclear family and companionate marriage were indeed inventions of this period is intelligently reviewed in Naomi Tadmor's, *Family and Friends in Eighteenth-Century England* op. cit., which makes a persuasive case for thinking about the 18th Century English family in terms of ideas of household, kinship and friendship distinctive to contemporaries. Tadmor's argument that the

spousal affection, moreover, opened up the prospect of a contractual version of marriage based on choice, in which both parties entered the marital contract as full legal (juridical) subjects. But this potentially contractual view of marriage was in tension with the emerging role of family life in marking social distinctions and stabilising gender relations from the mid-18ᵗʰ Century on; and this tension, as we shall see, found vivid expression in novels.

The early part of this period gave birth to Defoe's second (and final) female heroine, *Roxana* (1724). Roxana, like Moll, is an attractive and talented woman who, when abandoned by her first husband, divests herself of the encumbrance of her children and becomes the mistress of a well-to-do jeweller. On his death, she manages matters so as to inherit a substantial fortune. This she increases by assuming, *ancien régime* style, the marks of status which money can buy, taking up a life as a (very...) high class courtesan before, finally and reluctantly, settling for marriage with a Dutch merchant once her market power as a courtesan seems likely to diminish.

For our purposes, the most significant thing about the novel—particularly in the light of John Zomchick's claim that the 18ᵗʰ Century novel was importantly concerned in the construction of the idea of 'juridical subjectivity', and that this legal, contractual and individual subject status was being explored particularly in the context of familial and property relations[79]—is Roxana's critique of marriage. In essence, she regards marriage as a bad bargain—a contract which no rational woman would make. And she has the confidence to negotiate about it with her would-be husband, asserting her right to live the identity of an independent 'she-merchant'. Of particular interest is a fascinating scene in which Roxana debates the sexual politics of marriage with the Dutch merchant, of whom she is fond and who wants to marry her. It is true that she is put off the marriage by the not inconsiderable problem her first husband may still be alive. But Defoe makes it clear that a far stronger barrier is that she does not want to give up her wealth to a man.

18ᵗʰ Century (highly gendered) conception of friendship spanned both family and (a subset of) what we would today call 'friends' is of particular interest in the context of my argument about women's capacity to operate outside the home as the 'separate spheres' ideology discussed in the next section began to have some influence.

[79] John P. Zomchick *Family and Law in Eighteenth Century Fiction* op. cit.

When the merchant offers spontaneously to make a marriage settlement which lets her preserve control of her fortune, she is too embarrassed to admit that this was her motivation for refusal, and she therefore constructs a feminist argument about matrimony as inimical to liberty—an argument taken in substance from Mary Astell's *A Serious Proposal to the Ladies* (1694):[80]

'I told him, I had, perhaps, differing Notions of Matrimony, from what the receiv'd Custom had given us of it; that I thought a Woman was a free Agent, as well as a Man, and was born free, and cou'd she manage herself suitably, might enjoy that Liberty to as much Purpose as the Men do; that the Laws of Matrimony were indeed, otherwise, and Mankind at this time, acted quite upon other Principles, and those such, that a woman gave herself entirely away from herself in Marriage, and capitulated only to be, at best, but an Upper Servant. That the very Nature of the Marriage-Contract was, in short, nothing but giving up Liberty, Estate, Authority, and every-thing, to the Man, and the Woman was indeed, a meer woman ever after, that is to say, a Slave.'[81]

Roxana's would-be husband immediately responds with an argument about the division of labour:

'that the Man had all the Care of things devolv'd upon him; that the Weight of Business lay upon his Shoulders, and as he had the Trust, so he had the toil of Life upon him... that the Woman had nothing to do, but to eat the Fat, and drink the Sweet; to sit still, and look round her; be waited on, and made much of; be serv'd and loved, and made easie, especially if the Husband acted as became him...'

It is worth noting that this argument is not so much rooted in a view about the appropriateness of the status of wifehood to women as in a contractual argument that women get the better deal. Anticipating an assertion made by significant numbers of his 20th Century counterparts, the merchant declares that: 'In general the Women had only the Care of managing, that is spending what their Husbands get....' Not to be outdone, Roxana returns 'that while a woman was single, she was a masculine in her politick Capacity; that she had then the full Command of what she had, and the full Direction of what she did; that she was a man in her

---

[80] I am grateful to Philip Pettit for drawing this close analogy to my attention.

[81] *Roxana or, The Fortunate Mistress* (1724: op. cit. this and the following quotations are taken from pp. 148–9).

separated Capacity, to all Intents and Purposes that a Man could be so to himself.'; but if she marries 'all is the Interest, Aim, and View of the Husband; she is to be the passive Creature you spoke of...'. And so it goes on, with the merchant arguing for men's honour to women, and Roxana objecting that she doesn't want to be subject to a man's discretionary power. In 1724, Moll's equally luminous literary sister insists on her right to be not only a 'She-Merchant' but a 'Man-woman'.[82]

At one level, this is a very modern debate: in slightly different language, Roxana's critique of marriage would not look out of place in a late 20th Century feminist text. But here it is located within Wahrman's *ancien régime* world of cross-dressing, of 'breeches roles' in the theatre where women play men;[83] the world of the fop, the rake, and the Amazon. And it is a world in which this fluidity is producing an anxiety which itself contributes to the construction of new sets of norms, particularly those relating to masculinity and femininity. For women, the ultimate breach of the emerging gender norms consists in the sexual expressiveness (let alone assertiveness) invited by the very celebration of emotion intrinsic to the culture of sensibility; verbal wit and decisive activity are not necessarily frowned on in themselves, but constantly court a judgment of (immoral) lack of taste and discretion.[84] For men, effeminacy and lack of prudent judgment and self-restraint, as well as vulgarity towards women, are the main risks, in a world which regarded commercial culture as potentially feminising, and which saw a reassertion of sex difference as a way of avoiding, through a proper cultivation of sensibility, the vulgarising effects of commerce.[85] And

---

[82] The latter claim is made in Roxana's discussion with her financial adviser Sir Robert; 'I knew no State of Matrimony but what was, at best, a State of Inferiority, if not of Bondage; that I had no Notion of it that I liv'd a Life of absolute Liberty now; was free as I was born, and having a plentiful Fortune, I did not understand what Coherence the Words Honour and Obey had with the Liberty of a Free Woman....And seeing Liberty seem'd to be the Men's Property, I wou'd be a Man-woman; for as I was born free, I woul'd die so' (p. 171). On p. 131 she further refers to herself, in relation to managing her investments, as 'as expert in it, as any She-Merchant of them all'.

[83] Wahrman, *The Making of the Modern Self* op. cit. Chapters 1, 2, 4.

[84] See Frances Burney's *Camilla* (1796: op. cit.) for an extreme representation of the norms of feminine comportment and the pitfalls attendant on them: both Mrs Berlinton's excessive emotional sensibility and Mrs Arlbery's confident wit and contempt for public opinion lead them into breaches of the sexual code.

[85] G.J. Barker-Benfield, *The Culture of Sensibility* op. cit. Chapters 2 and 3: Harriet Guest, *Small Change* op. cit. Chapter 1: see in particular p. 47, p. 296.

these new virtues are in service of the protestant ethic which, as Watt observes,[86] is central to Defoe's world-view, yet which depends on a notion of social order very different from that which animates *Moll Flanders* or *Roxana*. And, sure enough, Defoe's admiration for Moll's and Roxana's Amazonian qualities duly gives way to a persistent critique of assertive, 'masculine' women in novels from *Clarissa* on.

Increasingly, the role which is developing amid the culture of sensibility—an extension of rather than a complete rupture with women's long-standing role in policing social honour, but a significant change nonetheless—confronts women with structural contradictions wherever their reason dictates some decisive action in relation to property or other autonomous conduct in the public world. And this is particularly evident in the sphere of marriage and family relations. An excellent example here—and it is no accident that she is the creation of a woman who had faced enormous personal difficulties in exercising her creative talents—is Frances Burney's *Cecilia*. Cecilia, an orphan, is wealthy, beautiful, intelligent and refined. She is also in an impossible position. First, her wealth is controlled during her minority by three variously despotic, dissolute or dangerous male guardians; second, her ultimate access to that wealth is contingent, should she wish to marry, on her husband's agreeing to take her name. Cecilia lacks neither rational faculties, nor intelligence: she is not, in principle, short of money. What she lacks is a world in which she can exercise these faculties with a reasonable degree of dominion. The expectations of society, as well as her own emotional attachments, tell her to marry; but the condition which her father has attached to marriage contradicts one of the founding principles of patriarchal social organisation. Cecilia is, simply, blocked by her social and legal situation: and though she and her lover do find a sort of escape, it is tremendously to Burney's credit that the novel has something much more subtle than a happy ending.

Nor were control of property and choice of marriage partner the only areas in which women experienced powerlessness in the family context. As the culture of sensibility gained ground, their responsibilities for exemplary conduct in the role of motherhood became particularly constraining. Significantly, during the last

---

[86] *The Rise of the Novel* op. cit. Chapters III and IV.

decade of the 18th Century, child-murder came, for the first time, to be regarded as a specifically female vice,[87] in a development which, as we shall see in the next chapter, had large consequences for the literary depiction of female criminality. Moreover the liberalisation of family law and policy—as enacted by the French revolutionary regime—became strongly associated with female depravity, in a distinctive gendering of the century-long tradition of English Francophobia.[88] It is accordingly no surprise that the impossibility of a woman's adequately discharging her maternal responsibilities under current power relations between the sexes is a central theme in novels by more radical writers—notably in Mary Wollstonecraft's *Maria*.[89]

The novel's didactic purpose—even in the hands of women, and even when tempered with a semi-ironic commentary—has now become trained on disciplining the expression of the female emotion on which it depends, and which it celebrates, through powers of judgment and discretion. The new protocols of credibility are hence heavily gendered.[90] In 1752, Charlotte Lennox's *Female Quixote* (a book in which female activity is explicitly labelled 'masculine') finds her eccentric romantic individualism held up to ridicule and ultimately tamed by a rationalist perspective delivered in the voice of a clergyman.[91] In 1791, Elizabeth Inchbald engineers the punishment of the coquetry of the enticing Miss Milner at the hands of her implacable and ferociously repressed guardian/husband Dorriforth/Lord Elmwood—a punishment the better part of which, like Clarissa, she herself regards as justified, signifying a tendency for even women novelists not only to punish women's transgression

---

[87] Josephine McDonagh, *Child Murder and British Culture 1720–1900* op. cit. p. 69; for an interesting discussion of the place of Mary Wollstonecraft's novel, *Maria* (1798: op. cit.) in both attracting, and criticising, a distinctive misogyny produced in part by conservative English reactions to the French Revolution, which had relaxed the laws of marriage, divorce and legitimacy, see pp. 85–8.

[88] Ibid, pp. 80–8.

[89] (1798: op. cit. 1798: cf. Mary Hays, *Memoirs of Emma Courtney* (1796: op. cit.).

[90] As well as being marked by social status. As Jan-Melissa Schramm puts it in relation to the 'gendered competition for credibility' in *Clarissa*, 'The struggle for power, and indeed the competition for testimonial creditworthiness, between the sexes and between the adherents to different economic codes, is...situated in the space between appearances and "reality"...'; *Testimony and Advocacy in Victorian Law, Literature and Theology* op. cit. pp. 83, 85.

[91] (1752: op. cit.): pp. 71, 125–6; the homily delivered by the clergyman is thought by some scholars to have been written by Lennox's friend and admirer Samuel Johnson.

but to make women in some sense take responsibility for their own punishment.[92] And in 1801,[93] Maria Edgeworth's Lady Delacour is punished physically for her bad wifehood and rejection of motherhood in the telling metaphor of a diseased breast.[94] Her subversion of the proper norms of femininity leads her into the embraces of, serially, unsuitable flirtations, quack doctors, and an over-emotional Methodism from which the ultimate escape, predictably, is a submission to marital authority, while her erstwhile, breeches-wearing, gender-bending friend, the tellingly named Harriet Freke, is roundly condemned. Of course, men's comportment too was regulated by the new manners: Henry Mackenzie's celebrated, unworldly and sentimental 'man of feeling' (1771), already gently but affectionately satirised in Goldsmith's *Vicar of Wakefield* (1766), gradually gives way to self-contained males such as Frances Burney's Edgar Mandelbert and Jane Austen's Colonel Brandon, whose communicative powers, such as they are, are models of reserve and indirection.[95] The depicted world of many late 18th Century novels is one in which norms of communication between the sexes—even within marriage—are so exquisitely confining as to engender in the modern reader a sense of suffocating claustrophobia[96] (though the same norms do, admittedly, give novelists a rich formal device for framing plots based on mutual incomprehension leading to misunderstandings which propel the action, of which both Frances Burney and Jane Austen are supreme exponents). And at a material level, these confining norms of comportment and communication also have an important bearing on the terrain over which women are allowed to act, as we shall see in the next section.

[92] Elizabeth Inchbald, *A Simple Story* (1791: Oxford World's Classics 1988).
[93] In *Belinda* op. cit.
[94] See Ruth Perry, 'Colonising the Breast: Sexuality and Maternity' *Journal of the History of Sexuality* (1991) 204 34.
[95] See Thomas Mackenzie's *The Man of Feeling* (1771: op. cit.); Oliver Goldsmith, *The Vicar of Wakefield* (1766: op. cit.); Frances Burney's *Camilla* (1796: op. cit.); Austen's *Sense and Sensibility* (1811 op. cit.). In Goldsmith's and, particularly, Mackenzie's books, there is some uncertainty about the degree to which the reader is invited unambiguously to celebrate the credulity and exquisite sensitivity which are the distinguishing features of the sentimental hero.
[96] Cf. W.B. Carnochan's analysis of the theme of confinement in 18th Century literature: *Confinement and Flight* (Berkeley: University of California Press 1977)—a confinement represented not only by the prisons of *Tom Jones*, *The Vicar of Wakefield*, *Roderick Random*, *Camilla* or *Caleb Williams*, but also by the domestic sphere of several of these novels, notably *Tom Jones* (in relation to Sophia's late mother) and *Camilla* (in relation to norms of communication).

It is in this context that education, and the invocation of a residual self capable of reflecting on experienced sensations and of learning to master or discipline them, becomes so important.[97] Just as Jane Austen made Sir Thomas Bertram agonise, at the end of *Mansfield Park*,[98] on the role of a deficient upbringing in spoiling his daughter Maria's character, and as George Eliot comments in *Middlemarch*[99] on the role of an indulgent and undisciplined upbringing on Fred and Rosamond Vincy, and on the role of different gender expectations in shaping that impact variously on the two of them, so Richardson is already meditating on similar themes in mid-18th Century *Clarissa*. In her last letter to her father, the heroine—wronged by her family as much as by her seducer—nonetheless thanks him for the upbringing which has taught her the path of virtue: '...let me bless you, my honoured papa... for all the benefits I have received from your indulgence... for the virtuous education you gave me; and for the crown of all, the happy end, which, through Divine grace, by means of that virtuous education, I hope, by the time you will receive this, I shall have made.' Similarly, her abductor Lovelace, in a late letter to his friend (and reformed rake) Belford, excoriates his mother for spoiling him *'Why, why did my mother bring me up to bear no control? Why was I so educated as that to my very tutors it was a request that I should not know what contradiction or disappointment was? Ought my mother not to have known what cruelty there was in her kindness?'*[100] And

---

[97] A topic which was central to the writings of not only Wollstonecraft but also Maria Edgeworth and her father: see Harriet Guest, *Small Change* op. cit. pp. 294–5.

[98] First published 1814; (Penguin Classics 1996) pp. 419–20.

[99] Op. cit; see for example pp. 328–9; 647.

[100] *Clarissa* op. cit. pp. 482, 499; emphasis in the original. This is not to say that the theme of essential goodness and evil had disappeared from novels at this time, even beyond the Gothic novels which feature plentiful models of 'natural' depravity. For example Elizabeth Inchbald's *Nature and Art* (1794: Teddington: The Echo Library 2006) uses the device of two brothers to ponder the relationship between nature and art—terms which are pervasive in the fiction of this period—in a framework which prefigures Romantic visions of good and evil as rooted in nature. Yet the book also depicts the influence of environment, notably in the figure of Agnes, who is driven to prostitution, theft and contemplated infanticide through lack of money and character in the harsh urban setting of London. In a telling anticipation of 19th Century themes, her eloquent plea to the legal authorities for mercy for the sake of her child is regarded as a symptom of derangement: see p. 85. The condemning judge's own condemnation is sealed by the fact that he is, unbeknownst to himself, the father of Agnes' child.

this concern with education—with the formation of character, depending on an essential core of inner selfhood characteristic of the emerging modern regime of identity—was, as we shall see in the next chapter, to become a cornerstone of early Victorian social and criminal policy.

From *Roxana* to *Fanny Price*: The Ideology and Reality of 'Separate Spheres'

The 18th Century novels, then, are reflecting a transition: a transition from a world in which notions of individual psychology are already apprehended as important—a world of dawning individualism; and yet a world in which that individualism is not yet possible to transcribe onto the status-based institutions of civil society, which are themselves changing slowly.[101] With Pamela's marriage in 1740, and Clarissa's birth and untimely death in 1748 (as untimely as a mere seven volumes would allow...), Moll Flanders was decisively buried, and female experimentation was confined within an increasingly inhibiting set of social norms. But what were the implications for women's treatment within the disciplinary institutions of the criminal process? The cult of sensibility and the re-emerging notion of fixed sexual difference and role issued in a whole series of changes in the treatment of women in criminal justice—the gradual (and without any legislative mandate) abandonment of public whipping of women during the 18th Century significant among them.[102] And beyond these direct effects, my suggestion is that the gradual hold which the culture of sensibility had on the perception of women would have had a significant effect on expectations about women's deviance, and hence on both levels of prosecuting crime and the treatment of women coming to the notice of the criminal process. It would therefore help to explain the apparent 'leniency' to women noted at every level of the

---

[101] Cf. the inability of the criminal justice system at this time to handle elaborated notions of capacity-based responsibility as an object of proof: see Chapter I.

[102] See Peter King, *Crime and Law in England* op. cit. pp. 53, 192–3; 269–74; see also V.A.C. Gatrell, *The Hanging Tree* op. cit. pp. 336–7; Martin Wiener, *Men of Blood: Violence, Manliness and Criminal Justice in Victorian England* op. cit. The legislative abolition of whipping of women did not come until 1817.

process from the second half of the 18th Century in King's detailed analysis of figures from several regions,[103] as well as why Feeley's and Little's data show a substantial decline in the representation of women in figures of recorded crime as early as the mid-18th Century. The intensified mechanisms of formal and particularly sexual control imposed on women, in other words, found their origins far earlier than the era of Victorian morality and its separate spheres ideology.

But this hypothesis suffers from an obvious weakness. The images of women which pervade the novel—like the writers and readers of novels—are largely drawn from the polite and middling classes. What, then, is their relevance for the treatment of a group of people who, as all the evidence shows, were disproportionately drawn from the labouring classes, from the itinerant poor and vagrants, and from the urban marginal or destitute? The argument rests on a fact observed in the previous chapter: that the novel-reading classes were precisely those in whose hands law enforcement, at almost every level, lay; hence their perceptions mattered fundamentally to the administration of the system and to outcomes within it. In short, if the world presented to readers of novels showed women to be weaker and less dangerous than men, we would expect to find this reflected in the perception of women's conduct as worthy—or unworthy—of formal action in the criminal process. And we might further expect that this emerging economy of gender difference—which, in the literary examples we have seen, had the effect of disciplining women in an inhibiting way—gave women, as the other side of its coin, a new language of comportment in which to signal their conformity and lack of threat. It helps, in other words, to put cultural flesh on the bones of King's conclusion that 'female offenders may simply have been perceived as less of a threat'.[104]

But this new signalling power applied, crucially, only to women who conformed to the code of polite feminine manners and sexual purity, enacting the newly fixed notion of essential identity produced by Wahrman's 'modern regime', which brought with it as an ironic counterpart of its interior individualism a need to stabilise the world in terms of racial, sexual and other categories. For those unable, for reasons of wealth, inclination or caste, to establish these

---

[103]   *Crime and Law in England* op. cit. Chapter 5.
[104]   Ibid, p. 192.

credentials of comportment, we would expect to find a 'tipping point', in which the lack of signalling opportunities available to the majority (and not only to those with significant funds, but also to the 'respectable poor'), would instantly mark them as unable to establish their veracity within the prevailing system of credibility, and hence as worthy of social control. This in turn would lead to a polarisation between two (numerically unequal) groups of women, and to relatively impermeable boundaries blocking the capacity of those who do not have signalling capacities to join the ranks of those who do. These are, I think, plausible if speculative hypotheses. But they cannot be made anything more than speculative without being articulated within a more concrete account of the material—economic and political as well as cultural and social— changes which were affecting women's lives in the second half of the 18ᵗʰ Century. It is to this subject that I now turn.

A huge amount has been written, by both historians and contemporary observers, about the emergence of capitalism and of urban society in late 17ᵗʰ and 18ᵗʰ Century England, and about the implications for social order. Moll's own criminality appears to reflect rather accurately what we know about female crime in the late 17ᵗʰ Century. It often involved the theft of valuable textiles and other articles of domestic equipment; women were well represented among receivers and pawnbrokers; levels of female property crime in London were relatively high, and a cause of significant anxiety; and women tended to work either alone or with other women, rather than with men.[105] Indeed, Moll's downfall is her impulsive decision to steal a horse: this being a form of thieving dominated by men, she had no access to the networks of trading which would have allowed her to dispose of the horse.[106] So even for Moll, gender-bending leads to trouble. Equally, literary observations about the role of women in policing reputation fit with emerging understandings of women's role in propagating social order in early modern England. Recent research has begun to reveal the relatively active part which women played, as litigants as well as witnesses and victims, even across such ostensibly

[105] See Walker, 'Women, Theft and the World of Stolen Goods' op. cit.; J.M. Beattie, 'The Criminality of Women in Eighteenth Century England' op. cit. p. 228.
[106] See Walker, *Crime, Gender and Social Order* op. cit. pp. 167–8.

inhospitable terrain as the administration of laws on witchcraft.[107] With the gradual privatisation of women in the Victorian era, and yet further with their supposed mental incapacities as socially determinist and biologistic theories of crime developed in the latter part of the 19th Century, it has been argued that criminal justice became displaced, less necessary, as a mechanism of women's social control. As Feeley and Little put it, the social, economic and cultural changes which accrued up to the late 19th Century may have meant that 'women became less inclined and able than men to engage in activity defined as criminal, and women were less subject to the criminal sanction as other forms of more private control emerged.'[108] King and Beattie, too, have noted the material implications of these cultural and economic changes for women, who 'formed a relatively small and declining proportion of property offenders in the late eighteenth and early nineteenth centuries. They also tended to be concentrated in types of crime such as petty larceny and shoplifting which were not felt to be particularly threatening or dangerous. They posed, to quote John Beattie, "a less serious threat to lives, property and order".'[109]

Driving changing patterns of female crime or perceptions of female criminal capacity, on this view, was the changing material position of women amid the relative decline of the agricultural economy in which they were securely integrated, and amid the emerging culture of sensibility, which accorded them a leading role in the process of civilisation and refinement of manners which was conceived as a counter to the corrupting effects of modernisation and urbanisation which we have seen reflected in literary plots. And—as reflected in both Feeley and Little's original article and in King's critical rejoinder—the established position among historians from the first glimmers of interest in women's history until the

[107] Walker, *Crime, Gender and Social Order* op. cit. Chapter 6, which develops the theme of women's agency, their active deployment of the legal process in areas like resisting distraint of goods, in exercise of their household authority, and pursuing bastardy cases. Throughout the book, Walker demonstrates the inaccuracy of stereotypes of stable masculine and feminine treatment and behaviour. See also Jim Sharpe, 'Women, Witchcraft and the Legal Process', Chapter 5 of Kermode and Walker (eds.), *Women, Crime and the Courts* op. cit.; and the editors' Introduction.

[108] 'The Vanishing Female' op. cit. p. 741; see also David F. Greenberg, 'The Gendering of Crime in Marxist Theory' op. cit. pp. 421–9.

[109] King, *Crime and Law in England* op. cit. p. 192, quoting Beattie, *Crime and the Courts in England* op. cit. pp. 240, 439.

last fifteen years or so had it that the industrialising and urbanising economy was bad news for women. It drew them in disproportionate numbers into the cities, where they found themselves in the most insecure sectors of the emerging economy: in sweated home labour; in poorly paid positions in factories; in domestic service where losing your character meant losing your livelihood; or in the workhouse or brothel. Of significance to my argument about polarisation and a 'tipping point' of inability to signal respectability reached by the excluded minority is the fact that women have been estimated to have made up over 80% of those classed as poor for much of the second half of the 18th Century.[110] As the cultural changes which accentuated a sense of fixed sex difference took hold, and as forms of labour in which women had long been well represented began to change, men seized the initiative and had the best of the bargain. There emerged, in short, an increasingly sexually separated pair of social and economic spheres.[111]

More recently, in the context of a general reappraisal of the idea of a sudden and culturally as well as economically decisive industrial revolution, many historians have been substantially revising this so-called 'separate spheres' account.[112] They have pointed out that the mid- and late 18th Century was also a time of burgeoning opportunity for (at least relatively privileged) women; with rising literacy and rising political participation not only in the person

[110] See Richard Connors, 'Poor Women, the parish and the politics of poverty', in Barker and Chalus, *Gender in Eighteenth Century England* (London: Longman 1997) pp. 127, 138.
[111] The classic statement of this argument is to be found in Leonore Davidoff and Catherine Hall, *Family Fortunes: Men and Women of the English Middle Class, 1780–1850* (London: Hutchinson 1987), a book which emphasises the cultural association of female domesticity with emerging, middle class notions of respectability which engendered novel ideas of proper feminine character.
[112] See Amanda Vickery, 'Golden Age to Separate Spheres? A Review of the Categories and Chronology of English Women's History' 36 *The Historical Journal* (1993) 412, an article whose challenge to the idea of a smooth developmental trajectory has had a lasting impact on the field. For other important contributions, see Hannah Barker and Elaine Chalus, *Gender in Eighteenth Century England* (London: Longman 1997), in which the main literature in the original analysis of separate spheres and more recent revisionist accounts is helpfully reviewed by the editors (see pp. 8–24); and Boyd Hilton, *A Mad, Bad, and Dangerous People? England 1783–1846* (The New Oxford History of England: Oxford University Press 2006) pp. 353–71 and in a thorough and judicious annotated bibliography on pp. 688–90. See also G.J. Barker-Benfield, *The Culture of Sensibility* op. cit. Chapters 4–6; Robert Shoemaker, *Gender in English Society 1650–1850: The Emergence of Separate Spheres?* op. cit.

of spectacularly intelligent women like Georgiana, Duchess of Devonshire or Mary Wollstonecraft but also in the much more numerous women who attended the many—some of them all-female—debating societies which flourished in the teeming civil society of 18th Century London.[113] Both the 'Bluestocking Circle' of the second half of the Century and, later, writers like Austen, Burney and Edgeworth, as well as feminists like Wollstonecraft and even Evangelicals like Hannah More, proclaimed women's intellectual capabilities. In their different ways, all of them tried to counter what was undoubtedly a backlash against the assertions of female independence and political activity which had been toler-ated in the first half of the Century, helping to engender a cul-tural context in which women could gradually come to think of themselves as political beings.[114] (It is worth remembering that the formal bar on women's political participation came, ironically, only with the first Reform Act of 1832: up to this point, women who were ratepayers were eligible to vote in local elections.[115]) Women were also finding their ways into new sectors of the economy, with increasing literacy meaning, for example, that numbers of women teachers in the burgeoning female academies were growing mark-edly over the period.[116] Nor were women absent from businesses engaged in small-scale production and services: though their scale meant that they accounted for a significant proportion of the work-force, very large industrial employers remained, right up to the late 19th Century, the exception rather than the rule, and widowhood or marital cooperation meant that, as Hannah Barker has shown, women were actively involved in running small businesses in many areas of the country.[117]

---

[113] See Elaine Chalus, 'That epidemical Madness: women and electoral politics in the late eighteenth century', and Amanda Foreman, 'A politician's politician: Georgiana, Duchess of Devonshire and the Whig party', pp. 151 and 179 respect-ively of Barker and Chalus op. cit.; on debating societies, see Donna Andrew, *London Debating Societies 1776–1799* (London Record Society 1994) http://www.british-history.ac.uk/source.asp?pubid=238.

[114] The contributions of some of these individuals have already been discussed; on cultural attitudes to women's learning through the Century, see Harriet Guest, *Small Change* op. cit., Part II of which deals with the Bluestocking Circle.

[115] See Robert Shoemaker, *Gender in English Society* op. cit. Chapter 6.

[116] Susan Skedd, 'Women teachers and the expansion of girls' schooling in England, c. 1760–1820', p. 101 of Barker and Chalus op. cit.

[117] Hannah Barker, *The Business of Women: Female Enterprise and Urban Development in Northern England 1760–1830* (Oxford University Press 2006); and

This recent reappraisal of the separate spheres argument has much to recommend it—not least in its unanswerable reminder that prevailing social ideologies are not identical with prevailing social practices. Clearly, late 18th Century women were not strictly confined to the domestic sphere: indeed, they were out in public—shopping,[118] in malls and gardens, at the theatre, as well as in a number of political and working contexts—to a much greater degree than would have been typical in an agricultural economy based on home work. The static rural world had, after all, been characterised for most people by low levels of wealth and relatively constrained social networks: there were infrequent public events beyond the wedding, christening or funeral, and few opportunities for consumption beyond the male-dominated space of the inn.[119]

Nevertheless, the separate spheres argument remains persuasive. First, it is generally acknowledged that, notwithstanding the difficulties of computation, women constituted a lower proportion of those in paid employment by the second half of the 19th Century than they had in the late 18th Century—a very surprising fact in the context of capitalist growth and development.[120] And notwithstanding their activity in the area of business, they made up a very small minority, as Barker's own study shows. Second, consider the fate of even spectacularly talented and educated women like the Duchess of Devonshire or Mary Wollstonecraft. Their agency and intelligence was widely recognised; yet when their comportment flouted established norms—in Devonshire's case, both gender- and class-bending by public appearances on the electoral hustings, as opposed to behind the scenes; in Wollstonecraft's case, engaging in 'free love' and radical politics—their activities were severely criticised and, in Devonshire's case, curtailed, in Wollstonecraft's, vilified.[121] Even the

'Women, work and the industrial revolution: female involvement in the English printing trades', in Barker and Chalus op. cit. p. 81.

[118] See Harriet Guest, *Small Change* op. cit. Chapter 3.

[119] See G. J. Barker-Benfield, *The Culture of Sensibility* op. cit., Introduction.

[120] In particular, the number of married women holding jobs has been estimated to have dropped by more than 50% in the second half of the 19th Century: see Jane Lewis, *Women in England 1870–1950* (Bloomington: Indiana University Press 1984) p. 149.

[121] Particularly after her death: for an interesting analysis of her lover and later husband William Godwin's ill judged attempt to defend her reputation, see Barker-Benfield op. cit. Chapter 7. The attempt was marked by some striking gender stereotypes which would surely have appalled Wollstonecraft.

'feminization of patriotism' and the increasing willingness to regard women's learning as a source of national pride, persuasively charted by Harriet Guest,[122] had a double edge: such learning increasingly had to be deployed within the constraints of norms of proper comportment and subject matter. As Boyd Hilton puts it, 'the attempt to argue that women were politically significant can only go so far'.[123]

Women's material access to theoretically increasing opportunities was heavily circumscribed, in other words, by not only the social and legal impediments to education and financial independence but by conformity to constraining—and gendered—cultural norms. It was not merely a question of the diminution of the terrain over which women were allowed to act, but also an exquisite ratcheting up of the norms of comportment which conditioned their access to that terrain. And this, crucially for our argument, as will become apparent in the next chapter's analysis of the 19th Century, was just as true of domestic servants or agricultural workers as it was of aristocrats like the Duchess of Devonshire.

By the early 19th Century, then, Moll Flanders, having been upstaged in the femininity stakes by Pamela and then eclipsed by Clarissa, has been decisively superseded by Fanny Price. Witty or dominant women continue to appear in novels—notably in novels written by women—but they are now the object of the novel's didactic purpose, oriented to discipline and domestication. Women's bad behaviour is no longer epitomised by Moll's enterprising lawbreaking but by deficient or selfish manners, morals, or, above all, motherhood. The epitome of heroine status is, accordingly, no longer Defoe's she-merchant but Austen's would-be home-maker. But this is not a matter of feminine incapacity or will. Like Clarissa, Belinda, or Cecilia, Fanny Price is just as much an agent as Moll Flanders: she is just as rational, and, in her own way, just as strong. But the social terrain on which she is allowed to act has diminished to something approaching Jane Austen's famous 'little piece of ivory',[124] while the comportment which she must observe as she etches it must be every bit as controlled as the artist's

---

[122] *Small Change* op. cit. Part Three (on the relationship between patriotism and women's learning) and Part Four (on the impact of the culture of sensibility).

[123] *A Mad, Bad and Dangerous People? England 1783–1846* op. cit. p. 689.

[124] Letter from Jane Austen to J. Edward Austen, 16th December 1816, quoted in Claire Tomalin, *Jane Austen: A Life* (Revised edition, Harmondsworth: Penguin 2000) p. 263.

knife. By the time Fanny watches silently as almost everyone else in *Mansfield Park* behaves badly (and duly gets their just deserts...), the shade of Moll Flanders, the active, transgressive literary heroine of a century before, has paled to the point of invisibility. Women may still be regarded as agents but, as George Eliot puts it in the mouth of the embittered Mrs. Transome in *Felix Holt*, 'What is the use of a woman's will?' Even in the words of the more tractable Esther, 'A woman must choose meaner things, because only meaner things are offered to her.'[125]

[125] *Felix Holt* op. cit. pp. 374, 407. Interestingly, Esther's comment is a memory of something which she said earlier in the novel, but the two formulations are in fact different, with the first expressed in terms of determination rather than agency: 'She must take meaner things, because only meaner things are within her reach': see pp. vi–vi.

CHAPTER III

'The weaker half of the human family'?: responsibility, mind and morals in the age of Tess

'Never in her life—she could swear it from the bottom of her soul—had she ever intended to do wrong; yet these hard judgments had come. Whatever her sins, they were not sins of intention, but of inadvertence, and why should she have been punished so persistently?'[1]

So reflects Hardy's Tess of the d'Urbervilles as she is on the point, for the second time in her story, of capitulating to Alec d'Urberville's attempts at seduction. As a young girl, flattered by Alec's attentions, Tess puts herself in a vulnerable position which Alec exploits in a course of conduct which, by today's standards, would amount to rape. After continuing a relationship with him for some time, she returns to her home, pregnant, and bears a child who, to her intense distress, dies shortly thereafter. She then finds work, in a different area, as a milkmaid, where she meets the attractive, intelligent but, as it turns out, emotionally rigid Angel Clare. Angel presses Tess to marry him, which she ultimately does, though tortured by her failed attempts to tell him of her earlier seduction. When she finally tells him of it on their wedding night, Angel, in a spectacular instance of the sexual double standard, rejects her. Abandoned by Angel, in desperate financial circumstances because she is too proud to appeal to his parents, and haunted by the ruin of her family, forced to move from their home because of the social

---

[1] *Tess of the d'Urbervilles* op. cit. p. 370.

judgment upon her as 'not a proper woman',[2] Tess is about to give
way to Alec's renewed pressure that she should place herself under
his financial protection and, of course, sexual dominion. Her decision is to have fatal consequences. When Angel, finally apprised
of her desperate situation, and eager for a *rapprochement*, reappears,
Tess's dogged forbearance gives way. She kills Alec and follows
Angel, with whom she hides for a few days pending her inevitable
arrest, conviction and execution.

Tess's fate as a female offender was by this time a rare one. Between
1836 and 1899, only 18 women were hanged for murder of a husband,
and five of these executions took place between 1847 and 1852.[3] By
contrast, several hundred men were executed for wife-murder over
this period—a figure which represents, as Martin Wiener has argued,
significant changes in attitudes to male and female violence over the
19th Century. Yet Tess's situation, and her despairing words, encapsulate neatly the themes which mark the representation of transgressive
women in law and literature in a 19th Century world in which Moll
Flanders is a distant echo in cultural history, just as her real sisters
have taken up more modest roles before the criminal courts.

At the point at which we left our story at the end of the last
chapter, Tess, with her wayward yet intense subjectivity and her
hereditary impulsiveness, was still some way in the future. Even
within a criminal system primarily oriented to external markers of
responsibility within an enduring though modulating economy of
character, social and economic changes had already set up a situation conducive to the lesser criminalisation of women. Emerging
ideas of women's civilising role within the culture of sensibility
had produced an image of femininity which, spilling over from the
polite classes represented in the novels, rendered women in general less likely to be regarded as threatening and hence subject to
formal prosecution. The world of early capitalism had produced,
ironically, a gradual re-affirmation of fixed sexual difference, in
which women are, as it were, characterised as essentially less dan-
gerously transgressive than men. What happened next?

By the beginning of the 19th Century, where we take up the
story, the conventional wisdom has it that we have reached a point

---

[2] Ibid. p. 368.
[3] Martin Wiener, *Men of Blood: Violence, Manliness and Criminal Justice in
Victorian England* op. cit.

at which Wahrman's *'ancien régime* of identity' has been decisively
displaced by a 'modern regime' of unique and unified individual
selfhood. This is a world in which it is generally supposed that
the philosophical and social ideas of identity and responsibility are
firmly oriented to subjectivity and agency rooted in human capacities and in a psychological interior;[4] one in which the world of
'credit' has been displaced by an effort to assess individual credibility, itself founded in an inner authenticity; and one whose criminal
system is displacing patterns of manifest criminality in favour of
subjective or harm-based patterns. But what impact did this philosophical 'modern regime of identity' and associated developments
really have on legal conceptions of criminal responsibility and practices of responsibility-attribution? A change in prevailing social
ideas does not, after all, automatically realise itself completely across
social institutions, which continue, though inevitably marked by
their cultural environment, to be structured by relatively discrete
imperatives and capacities. Even if we grant that there was a general social movement towards psychological, intentionalist theories
of agency, therefore, we need to ask whether *criminal* responsibility
did come to take Tess's view that responsibility and punishment
should be premised on 'sins of intention' as opposed to 'sins of inadvertence'. And, to the extent that that was the case, there arises the
further question of how far this development displaced the reliance
on external markers of character which we saw in Chapters I and
II to have been so central to the operation of 18th Century criminal
justice.

We also need to examine the implications of developments in
ideas of moral and criminal responsibility for the treatment of
female offenders in law and literature. Was this a world in which
an increasing concern with the degrees of engaged human capacity,
reflected in attributions of intention, knowledge or self-control, was
leading to a yet lesser impulse to criminalise what Wilkie Collins

---

[4] It should be acknowledged that the word 'psychological' here is ana-
chronistic: on the history of psychology and in particular of the implications of
the practices of the 'psy' disciplines on human subjectivity, see Nikolas Rose,
Governing the Soul op. cit. A psychological understanding of human subjectivity
and conduct was, of course, developing unevenly over a long period, but as Rose
shows, its real impetus gathered in the 20th Century. On the distinctiveness of
the prevailing conceptions of 'psychological medicine' prevailing even in the late
19th Century, see Mariana Valverde, *Diseases of the Will: Alcohol and the Dilemmas
of Freedom* (Cambridge University Press 1998).

dubbed 'the weaker half of the human family',[5] and to reconceive female criminality, as Lucia Zedner has argued, in terms of biological or social pathology and sexual deviance? Or did conceptions of female agency survive, with women's slow decline in the numbers of recorded offenders mapping rather onto the materially polarising effects of the culture of sensibility and the consolidation of separating economic and social spheres in the sway of continuing capitalist and industrial development? Clearly, the vision of criminality represented by Tess is significantly different from that embodied in Moll Flanders; but did this imply a generalised conception of feminine weakness, or rather a distinctive framework for the discipline of women's will? Tess provides a useful case study, not only because her story is well known, but also because it sits precisely at the intersection between these various dynamics: she displays both agency and pathology, while her decisions and impulses are located by Hardy within a vividly sketched economic and social environment, distinguished by a punitive system of sexual discipline.

Within these broad themes, I will analyse examples of female transgression drawn from 19th Century novels against the backcloth of an intriguing argument recently advanced by legal and literary scholars. John Bender, Alexander Welsh, Jan-Melissa Schramm and Lisa Rodensky[6] have argued that from the late 18th Century and throughout the 19th Century there persisted an unusual parallel between criminal law and the genre of the novel in their mutual concern with individual responsibility. In the novel, an increasing preoccupation with psychological realism was being pursued by means of the formal device of the all-seeing narrator, reporting, *à la* Watt's realism of representation, characters' inner lives and motivations, but also commenting, *à la* Watt's realism of assessment, on the quality of character and conduct. And in the court room, judge, jury or Justice were increasingly required to make judgments about inner states of mind as a condition for the attribution of responsibility, while pondering the proper boundary between such subjective

[5] Wilkie Collins, *The Moonstone* (1868: Oxford World's Classics, 1999), p. 84; the reference is semi-ironic.

[6] John Bender, *Imagining the Penitentiary: Fiction and the Architecture of Mind in Eighteenth-Century England* op. cit.; Alexander Welsh, *Strong Representations: Narrative and Circumstantial Evidence in England* op. cit.; Jan-Melissa Schramm, *Testimony and Advocacy in Victorian Law, Literature and Theology* op. cit.; Lisa Rodensky, *The Crime in Mind: Criminal Responsibility and the Victorian Novel* op. cit.

conceptions of responsibility and objective standards based on the evaluation of the reasonableness of conduct and the propriety of character. As the Century wears on, Rodensky suggests, there is a shift in both novels and criminal law away from notions of objective responsibility and towards an exploration of purely subjective crim-inality. There were, of course, clear differences between the novel and the criminal law. In novels, the omniscient third party narra-tor, with unrestricted access to characters' inner reflections, resolves the problems of credibility which continue to perplex the law in a world of increasing mobility and an increasing belief in the idea that the clue to human motivations lies in a hidden human interior. In law, there was also the necessity of reaching a judgment and indeed of executing it—a difference which led some commentators, not-ably Fitzjames Stephen, to castigate the irresponsibility of writers who sought to use literary forms to 'try' real characters *in absentia*.[7] But the parallels are, Rodensky argues, close enough to suggest a common concern with a matter of salience to contemporaries.

Drawing on, but questioning some important aspects of Rodensky's thesis, I shall advance three main contentions. First, I shall argue that the turn to psychology and subjectivity was far from complete, and that for much of the 19th Century mechanisms of legal responsibility-attribution remained both fundamentally evaluative and importantly trained on external markers of character. Instead of any radical dis-continuity, in other words, what we see in the 19th Century is rather a continuing negotiation between capacity/psychology and charac-ter/evaluation in the attribution of criminal responsibility, between the worlds of credit and credibility, between realisms of represen-tation and assessment, between different resolutions of the problems of knowledge and virtue. And this, as I shall try to show, is clearly reflected in literary representations of criminality.

Second, I shall question the case for a supposed move towards a capacity-based pattern of subjective criminality in what might be thought to be its strongest terrain: situations in which questions of insanity or other forms of mental incapacity are at issue. It is often argued that 19th Century female criminality is being projected onto

[7] Sir James Fitzjames Stephen, *The Story of Nuncomar and the impeachment of Sir Elijah Impey* (1885: Cornell Lilbrary Digital Collections, http://www.library. cornell.edu); Stephen's essay is discussed in Rodensky, op. cit. Chapter 4: cf. Richard A. Posner's critique of law and literature scholarship: *Law and Literature: A Misunderstood Relation* (Cambridge: Harvard University Press 1988).

sexual deviance, madness and, later on, a group of social pathologies such as weak-mindedness or inebriety, ensuring women's criminal marginality within an 'economy of capacity' rather than an 'economy of character'. Yet both legal and literary evidence should lead us to modify this hypothesis. In literature, examples of female criminality are as often rooted in an analysis of social environment as of incapacity. And in law, the emerging exculpatory framework of insanity and associated defences, usually understood in terms of a process of gradual formalisation and medicalisation,[8] itself discloses for much of the 19th Century a strongly physicalist conception of mind and a model of judgment marked as much by a moral and common-sensical assessment of character and conduct as by a factual assessment of capacity or state of mind. As I shall try to show, this predominantly moral/ evaluative viewpoint, trained onto external markers of dangerousness which lie somewhere between 'manifest' and 'harm-based' patterns of criminality, is also strongly reflected in literary representations.

Furthermore, I shall suggest that the preoccupation with absence of mind in the literary representation of female crime, including that of Tess, signifies not so much a construction of madness but rather a troubling limit to both 'subjective' and 'objective' patterns of criminality. Just as Moll reflected a real concern about certain forms of urban female crime in the early 18th Century, so her successors stand in for attempts to ponder salient cultural perplexities. And in an era when Moll had become unthinkable, female deviancy may have been rendered more palatable to the Victorian imagination when represented as coinciding with moments of suspended agency. But the relevance of absence of mind was much broader than this. For, to the extent that a new, factual and psychological model of agency was taking hold, the epistemological question of how the reader or juror can make judgments where subjectivity is not unified, or where the source of criminality is beyond the conscious control or mind of the offender, would have been a particularly troubling one. As such, it is not surprising that it is a vivid theme not only for women, but also for men in literature. Note, however, that this perplexity does not arise exclusively within a subjective pattern of criminality; for absence of mind, like insanity, also unsettles mechanisms of objective liability by disrupting both the model of the reasonable person as a standard of judgment and the idea of natural consequences as intended.

---

[8] See Arlie Loughnan, *Mental Incapacity Defences in Criminal Law* op. cit.

Finally, I shall argue that Victorian conceptions of female deviancy reflected in the literary representation of women offenders, many of them 'flat' characters at the margins of novels, give us too narrow a perspective, and lead too readily to a view of deviant women as weak-minded non-agents. Since Moll's unthinkability is premised, as I argued in the last chapter, on the construction of an increasingly exquisite conception of female comportment, female deviance has come by the late 18th Century to consist not primarily in criminal conduct but in acts and attitudes of self-assertion inconsistent with prevailing norms of gender role or sexual propriety. When we include ambitious, non-conformist literary women within the category of female deviance, we can see more clearly that women's agency, while its exercise has been constrained, has not been buried, conceptually, with Moll. It is all too easy, in short, to exaggerate the degree to which the 19th Century witnessed a declining belief in women's agency across the board as opposed to among certain groups. A better analysis of women's fate in the process of criminalisation is rooted, as it was in relation to the late 18th Century, in an understanding of the implications of both cultural norms and economic practices for the treatment of distinct groups of women. Broadening the conception of female transgression in this way, I argue that perhaps the two most gifted and independent-minded 19th Century realist heroines, William Thackeray's Becky Sharp and George Eliot's Dorothea Brooke, stand as a powerful metaphor both for the difficulty in inserting autonomous female activity into an increasingly sexually divided world, and yet for the continued vitality of a cultural sense of women's agency.

From Evangelicism and Utilitarianism to Social Determinism: Subjective and Objective Principles of Responsibility in Victorian Criminal Law

As is well known, the first decades of the 19th Century saw the consolidation of the architecture of the modern English criminal process and of the adversarial trial system already glimpsed in the

second half of the 18th Century. This modernising era saw the creation of the police, the introduction of defence counsel, the refinement of rules of evidence and the repeal of many of the capital
statutes. This impressive, though incomplete, programme of reform
was shaped by two main intellectual influences which had found
an echo in English politics: the world-view which underpinned the
Evangelical revival of the end of the 18th Century,[9] and the broadly
utilitarian ideas reaching back to Adam Smith and Cesar Beccaria
and finding voice in London in the person of Jeremy Bentham.
Each of these, in their different ways, was challenging the received
wisdom, in criminal justice as elsewhere, of the landed aristocracy
whose power had underpinned the construction of the 'Bloody
Code' and discretionary 18th Century criminal justice. This system
was ill-suited to the management of criminal justice in the urban
setting which was closer to the concerns of the new bourgeois
interests so strongly represented in the novel.

On the face of it, the Evangelical and Utilitarian philosophies
could hardly have been more different. But in the context of criminal justice, as Martin Wiener has persuasively argued,[10] they coa-
lesced in an unlikely but stable equilibrium. The idea that the
criminal process should be designed so as to encourage remorse and
genuine repentance fitted rather well with the utilitarian notion
of deterrence, and came together in the early Victorian project of
punishment as geared to maximising offenders' capacity to work
on their characters.[11] What the subjective internalisation of responsibility, guilt and repentance was to achieve in the Evangelical
framework, the external incentives set up by the threat of punishment were to achieve within the system of utility. These 'internal'
and 'external' threads often combined in the thinking of opinion-
formers, notably Charles Dickens, whose widely read articles on
criminal policy were highly influential on popular opinion. An

---

[9] See Boyd Hilton, *A Mad, Bad, and Dangerous People? England 1783–1846* op.
cit. pp. 174–94.
[10] *Reconstructing the Criminal* (Cambridge University Press 1991); on evangelical
and utilitarian influences on early 19th Century criminal policy, see also Richard
R Follett, *Evangelicalism, Penal Theory and the Politics of Criminal Law Reform in
England, 1808–30* (Basingstoke: Palgrave 2001); Coleman Phillipson, *Three Criminal
Law Reformers: Beccaria, Bentham, Romilly* (London and Toronto: J.K. Dent and
Sons, 1923); K.J.M. Smith, *Lawyers, Legislators and Theorists* op. cit.
[11] An aspiration which John Bender has argued itself reflects the novel's con-
cern with reformation of character: *Imagining the Penitentiary* op. cit.

optimist about crime prevention through better social education, and a psychologically astute critic of the inhumanity of the separate system in prisons, Dickens was nonetheless a sceptic about reform through punishment: his preference was for (often harsh) incentive systems geared to deterrence. These views were reflected in his own intervention into ameliorative social policy, the hostel for 'fallen women' at Urania House.[12]

At the level of the notion of responsibility which had to be proven at trial, the successive reports of the Criminal Law Commissioners show that, for many would-be reformers, an increasing importance was being attached to advertence,[13] issuing in what Fletcher has famously described as a 'subjective pattern of criminality':[14] the idea that the essence of responsibility for crime lies in the offender's subjective mental state. Crucially, however, the idea which animated much early Victorian criminal policy—that human beings had the capacity to work on their characters—was entirely consistent with reliance on an objective principle of *mens rea*. A failure to attain a reasonable standard of care or attention, in the context of normal capacities, could be regarded as culpable—a reflection of the 'harm- or risk-based pattern of criminality' which Fletcher also notes, and which is vividly reflected in the expansion of summary offences, many of them of strict, no-fault liability, at mid-Century. And this harm- or risk-based pattern, rather than the pattern of subjective criminality, was certainly in the ascendant among the socially Darwinist, determinist and biological theories of criminality which began to surface, partially displacing the early Victorian notions of crime as evil or moral degeneracy, in the latter part of the Century.

At the level of the substantive criminal law, the systematising impulse of the early 19th Century expressed itself in a movement for codification which engendered a series of Criminal Law Commissions charged with the task of drafting a consolidated criminal code. There has been a tendency to write the history of 19th Century criminal law as if the Criminal Law Commissioners'

---

[12] Philip Collins, *Dickens and Crime* op. cit. Chapter 4: Dickens' acutely imaginative sympathy with the pain of isolation, reflected in the characterisation of Dr. Manette in *A Tale of Two Cities* (1859: Penguin Classics 2000), is discussed in Chapter 5.

[13] K.J.M. Smith, *Lawyers, Legislators and Theorists* op. cit.

[14] George P. Fletcher, *Rethinking Criminal Law* op. cit.

preference for advertence-based principles found direct expression in the law.[15] But the fact is that their reports were never implemented, and large-scale substantive legislation in the field of indictable offences mainly took the form of consolidations of existing common law. The formalisation of *mens rea*, accordingly, came slowly through case law, and many offences were—and remain—based on objective versions of *mens rea* such as negligence which did not require proof of advertence.[16] These objective principles, which are focused on assessments of moral character or of social danger, are of just as much importance in our understanding of the criminalisation of women as are the subjective principles which have enjoyed greater philosophical and historical attention. And standards of reasonableness, of course, would be likely to be strongly gendered. Hence sexual deviance as the typically feminine form of unreasonableness could readily become an important principle of criminalisation. Again, evaluations of character and risk of harm, rather than investigations of engaged subjective capacity, seem likely to have been in the ascendant.

Yet more importantly for an analysis of how far actual practices of criminal responsibility-attribution reflected a genuine assessment of subjective states, there is strong reason to think that the move to subjectivity was far from complete. As we saw in Chapter I, there were certainly institutional reasons for thinking this. Notable among them were the absence of a systematic appellate system capable of testing points of legal interpretation of doctrinal requirements, and the pervasiveness in the English system of lay justice in the hands of magistrates. The relative importance of such lay justice was in fact significantly increased with the huge expansion of the summary jurisdiction in the middle of the 19th Century. There is also compelling evidence that the system continued to rely on forms of 'local knowledge'—and accordingly to exhibit strong local variations—through to the end of the Century.[17] This may seem surprising given the increasing mobility implied by continuing industrialisation and urbanisation. Yet even in London, the

[15] See in particular K.J.M. Smith, *Lawyers, Legislators and Theorists* op. cit. Chapters 4 and 9.
[16] For a more detailed statement of this argument, see Nicola Lacey, 'In Search of the Responsible Subject: History, Philosophy and Social Sciences in Criminal Law Theory' op. cit.
[17] Carolyn Conley, *The Unwritten Law* op. cit.

epitome of the mobile and anonymous individualist world, there is plentiful evidence that dense social networks survived—a fact which is vividly reflected in the successive failures of slum clearances to generate a move, among the urban poor, to the suburbs.[18] Not only the difficulty and expense of travel into the centre where chances of work were highest, but also, significantly, the poor's reliance on networks of reputational and financial credit, made it preferable for them—to the consternation of successive policymakers—to tolerate the progressively grimmer overcrowding in the inner city rather than risk the social disembedding attendant on a move away to better housing.

But there is also a more specific, doctrinal reason for thinking that, even in cases where the ground for subjectivity was most fertile— the move to a psychological interpretation of 'malice aforethought' in murder being a key example—attributions of responsibility in the criminal courts may have been just as, or possibly even more focused on external as on internal markers: on objective evaluation than on assessment of subjective psychological states. This is the presumption that a person had intended the natural consequences of his or her acts. As an evidential presumption, this would be unremarkable: indeed, one might say that it is a fundamental of how we as human beings interpret one another. But, as I have argued in more detail elsewhere, there is reason to think that it often operated rather as a legal presumption.[19] In other words, for legal purposes, defendants simply *did* intend the natural consequences of their acts, unless some particular reason—an excusing state such as insanity for example— could be invoked to block the inference. At the level of judgment, this is objective: 'natural consequences' are not a factual but an evaluative matter. Would any reasonable person have seen this as a natural consequence? If so, the defendant is properly held accountable for it. Added to this, in the law of evidence, we have the ironic fact that the supposed era of subjective criminality was also the era in which the accused was virtually silenced, with the trial increasingly dominated by lawyers who were gradually constructing technical frameworks through which evidence had to be filtered to the jury.[20] At

---

[18] Gareth Stedman Jones, *Outcast London: A study in the relationship between classes in Victorian Society* (Oxford: Clarendon Press 1971) pp. 87–8 and Part II.

[19] 'In Seach of the Responsible Subject' op. cit.

[20] On the implications of this development for the relationship between law and literature, see John Bender, *Imagining the Penitentiary* op. cit. p. 176. The

doctrinal, evidential and process levels, then, there is strong reason to suppose that the 19th Century saw something much more complex than a linear move towards a pattern of subjective criminality founded on a factual assessment of the state of the defendant's mind.

Gendering the 'Residuum': The Criminalisation of Women in the 19th Century

Patterns of 19th Century criminality, then, remained focused on evaluative considerations even as the idea of subjective criminality was gaining ground among opinion-formers. What were the implications for women? Within the compass of this book, I can do no more than sketch the ways in which the many developments in criminal policy affected the situation of female offenders across the 19th Century. I am therefore fortunate to be able to draw on Lucia Zedner's meticulous analysis. Zedner charts an increasing emphasis on the female moral code whose origins we traced in the last chapter to the 18th Century, with women constructed as the guardians of family, of morals, and of motherhood. In this context, the notion of female deviance became strongly associated with women's sexuality—a situation reflected in the fact that the largest single group of women offenders already known to the police in the second half of the century (when reliable statistics for the purposes of gender comparisons became available) were prostitutes.[21] With social order in both urban and rural settings depending strongly on hierarchical female networks

vigorous debates about the uses and abuses of professional representation (on which see Cairns, *Advocacy and the Making of the English Criminal Trial 1800–1865* op. cit.), reflected in the famous 'War between the Bar and the Press' at mid-Century, were paralleled in the realist novel, with Dickens, Eliot, Gaskell and others taking up the question of how lawyers' wresting of control and displacement of the defendant's 'plain speech' distorted the evidential process, and lawyers conversely questioning the literary license of novelists: see Jan-Melissa Schramm, *Testimony and Advocacy in Victorian Law, Literature and Theology* op. cit. pp. 14–15, 55–6 and Chapter 3.

[21] For example, 28% of the women prosecuted in 1857 were charged with prostitution-related offences, declining to 12% in 1890: Zedner op. cit. p. 22.

of social control and shaming among the working classes, women themselves were involved in policing the norms of sexual respectability.[22] These prevailing gender norms had their impact on the criminalisation of women within the broader context of a slow development from a policy shaped primarily by moralism—both in its conception of crime as wickedness and in its conception of punishment as oriented to the amelioration of moral character. In the latter part of the century, however, this moralistic approach gave some ground to a tendency towards the pathologisation of certain categories of offender—the feeble-minded, the inebriate,[23] the habitual offender—several of them embracing important numbers of women.

Martin Wiener has suggested that this partial shift to a concern with the social and, later, biological determinants of offending may have been premised on the perceived successes of early Victorian criminal policy, which had mitigated the extreme fear of crime up to mid-century. In one of the first books to examine the links between Victorian literature and criminal policy, Philip Collins shows how this shift is reflected in Charles Dickens' representation of crime.[24] While Dickens' early novels like *Oliver Twist* (1837) tend to represent crime as committed by wicked characters, often in the context of an intensely threatening urban underworld, his later offenders—perhaps most notably Bradley Headstone in *Our Mutual Friend* (1865)—are explored as individuals whose criminality resides in pathological psychological disposition. And the intermediate figure of Hugh in *Barnaby Rudge* (1841) suggests the influence of upbringing and environment in shaping criminality, with Dickens inviting us to ponder whether Hugh's terrifying viciousness is innate, or the product of the cruel execution of his mother and his subsequent social abjection, or both.

As Zedner emphasises, however, it is important not to exaggerate the sense in which this was a shift from an evaluative to a scientific world-view. For the late Victorian discourses of criminal pathology were, like the discourse of 'mind doctors' of the era,

---

[22] Zedner op. cit. p. 16, citing Judith Walkowitz, *Prostitution in Victorian Society: Women, Class and the State* (Cambridge University Press 1980).
[23] See Mariana Valverde, *Diseases of the Will: Alcohol and the Dilemmas of Freedom* op. cit.
[24] Philip Collins, *Dickens and Crime* (2nd ed, London: Macmillan 1965) Chapter 11.

themselves heavily moralised.[25] This intertwining is perhaps most vividly exemplified in the famous debate about so-called 'moral insanity', a pseudo-medical concept which was applied with particular intensity to women. Zedner argues that moral insanity:

'equated mental health with virtue.... Though they might show no other sign of mental illness or defect, the "morally insane" were identifiable by the very fact of their persistently anti-social behaviour. In practice, "moral insanity", without ever being clearly defined, was widely used to denote a perceived moral incapacity... And it was in its application to the area of sexual non-conformity, especially in women, that the term gained its greatest credibility.'[26]

So while it is true that by the very end of the century, a tendency had grown up to regard habitual female offenders 'less as "bad" than as "mad"',[27] for most of the century the tendency was to rely on open-textured concepts such as 'moral insensibility', and hence to locate female criminality in the failings of properly female moral character rather than in psychological incapacity.[28]

From our point of view, perhaps the most interesting thing about concepts such as 'moral insanity' and 'moral insensibility' is the way in which they conflate conduct and character, focusing on external signals of danger or degeneracy rather than internal features of psychology and intentionality. And this continuing focus on character is reflected in a number of tangible institutional arrangements which Zedner tracks across the century. For example, the impressionistic category of the 'criminal classes'—i.e. those of bad reputation and/or with previous convictions, replaced in 1893 by the category of 'habitual offenders'—was regarded as hugely important

---

[25] As Ruth Harris has shown (*Murders and Madness: Medicine, Law and Society in the Fin de Siècle* (Oxford University Press 1989)), much the same *mélange* of medicine and moralism characterised debates about criminal responsibility in late 19th Century France.

[26] *Women, Crime and Custody* op. cit. p. 270.

[27] Zedner op. cit. p. 46.

[28] In passing, it is worth noting that the persistence of concepts such as 'moral insanity' puts a different spin on the 'turf wars' between doctors and lawyers charted by Roger Smith in his influential account of criminal insanity in 19th Century England (*Trial by Medicine* op. cit.). Smith argues that medicine and law were in competition because while law sought to make an evaluative judgment based on an assumption of responsibility, medicine sought to make a factual judgment on the basis of determinist assumptions. The moral insanity debate suggests that what was at issue was rather a pair of competing evaluations.

to the identifiability of those thought to be 'vicious in character', particularly in the cities. Given the polarisation of urban women's lives, a generalised perception of women as less dangerous than men, or as dangerous only in certain contexts or when bearing certain marks of character, would have fed into patterns of criminalisation. And, significantly, while women made up only about 20% of those estimated to belong to the 'criminal classes' in the latter half of the century for which reliable statistics are available,[29] a far smaller proportion of the women than of the men represented in the official statistics were categorised as being of previous good character. Across the period 1857–1893, women made up only about 12% of this category: in 1857, only 17% of women, as opposed to 36% of men, had no criminal record: and by 1890, 53% of men but only 35% of women in court were first offenders. As Zedner comments, 'The smaller proportion of women in this class may reflect the tendency to see women as non-criminal. If a female offender had no previous criminal record, efforts may have been made to keep her out of the criminal justice system. Conversely, after women had been convicted once, the greater stigma attached to criminal women made them particularly liable to find themselves again in confrontation with the law.'[30]

It is generally agreed that by the end of the 19th Century, recorded female crime was at a relatively low level, amounting to less than one fifth of the more serious offences triable before a jury. Yet these low levels of recorded female crime were juxtaposed with significant late Victorian fears of female criminality, and by a profusion of theories of female dangerousness, often projected onto images of sexually motivated or emotionally rooted crime.[31] It is worth contemplating the socio-economic context in which these fears of female crime developed and persisted. A useful resource here is Gareth Stedman Jones' classic study of the relationship between the

[29] Zedner op. cit. pp. 20–21; she estimates that this would have risen to something approaching 40% had vagrancy and prostitution not been excluded from 1860 on. The numbers of those classified within the criminal classes fell by half from 1860–90—an interesting index of both diminishing fears of crime and the increasingly targeted approach to criminal enforcement.

[30] Zedner op. cit. p. 22.

[31] See Lucia Zedner, *Women, Crime and Custody* op. cit. pp. 68ff; Judith R. Walkowitz, *Prostitution and Victorian Society: Women, class and the state* op. cit.; and, in relation to similar concerns about female criminal pathologies in France, Ruth Harris, *Murders and Madness: Medicine, Law and Society in the Fin de Siècle* op. cit.

social classes in London during the 19th Century: *Outcast London*. Though patterns of criminalisation in London became less distinctive after the mid-19th Century,[32] London remained an important focus for both the perception of crime problems and the development of criminal policy, not only because of the location of government and opinion-formers but also because the proportion of the population living there continued to rise, virtually doubling between 1821 and 1851, and doubling again between then and the end of the century.[33] Moreover London's focus as the object of fears of crime was accentuated by the anxieties about the corrupting effect of urban life which we saw reflected in the novels of the second half of the 18th Century, and by the perception that many of those migrating to London from the provinces were people of bad character: after all, if one had a secure place, the incentives to move would be assumed to be low.[34]

As an industrial centre, London was very different from northern cities such as Manchester or Newcastle. Much of its economy was focused on the production of high-quality finished goods like carriages, watches, jewellery, leather work or furniture within relatively small businesses rather than large factories. There was also a marked seasonality of production. This was attendant on population flows associated with the influence of the London 'season' on demand for consumer goods and services, and it was exacerbated by the influence of the weather on supplies coming from ports. Taken together, these factors produced a flexible labour market embracing a large pool of casual labour amid an economy which relied heavily on small-scale, often poorly paid, 'sweated' labour.[35] This predominance of an unskilled and insecure labour force promoted middle class fears about 'outcast London' throughout the 19th Century, and generated successive attempts to theorise the nature of what came to be known as the 'residuum'. These parallel closely theories of criminality, with socially Darwinist approaches partially displacing, from the 1880s, approaches grounded in theories of moral degeneracy.[36] And alongside the social theories there developed policies oriented to managing 'outcast London', notably

---

[32] Peter King, *Crime and Law in England* op. cit. pp. 217–8.
[33] Gareth Stedman Jones, *Outcast London* op. cit. p. 160.
[34] Ibid, p. 12.
[35] Ibid, pp. 20–38, pp. 83ff.
[36] Ibid, Chapter 16.

in the form of criminal policy, urban planning and the design and administration of the poor law—the latter an increasingly difficult problem as the well-to-do moved to the new suburbs, undermining the local fiscal basis for poor relief in the centre.[37]

Amid these attempts to comprehend and manage an increasingly disembedded and polarised urban society, the position of unskilled women emerged as particularly precarious. Unskilled or low-skilled female labour in domestic service or sweated industries like sewing was particularly vulnerable to fluctuations in demand and to the relentless reduction of wages attendant on those fluctuations. An especially large glut of female labour, accentuated by the lack of factory employment, led to very low average female wage rates, in contrast to rates of pay for skilled and some semi-skilled men, which were relatively high in London.[38] This meant that women married to these relatively secure men tended not to work—or did so only out of necessity in down times—implying a complete lack of female bargaining power even among the relatively well-to-do.

Adding to the concerns raised by women's fragile articulation with the economy, as the activities of female social policy reformers, campaigners for women's education and suffragists began to occupy a larger space in the public consciousness, the fear emerged that female liberation would spell higher female crime.[39] And throughout the 19th Century, women did in fact continue to be relatively well represented within certain sub-sectors of offending. For example, they made up a significant 30% of those charged with larceny under the value of five shillings until this category was abolished in 1879.[40] But these women, of course, were hardly among the ranks of the newly liberated woman, but rather of the urban poor—precisely the milieu in which women would find it hardest to recover markers of respectability once they had been

[37] Ibid, Chapter 13.

[38] Ibid, p. 83; the one exception here was female employment in factories making matches.

[39] Luke Owen Pike, *A History of Crime in England* Vol. 1 (London: Smith, Elder and Co. 1873) pp. 527–9.

[40] Zedner op. cit. p. 35; the other figures here are drawn from pp. 34, 37–40. Women also made up 20% of those charged with common assault, and 17% of summary offenders, among whom women were most often convicted of drunkenness. As compared with the figures for the property offences mentioned in the text, the latter figure is lower than one might have expected. This is perhaps to be explained by the orientation of many of the new summary offences to male-dominated work-related activities.

lost. Much the same must have been true of the women who made up 17% of summary offenders, among whom they were most often convicted of drunkenness; and, amid predominantly financially driven offending, the women who made up a third of those tried for forgery and two fifths of those tried for coining. And in the field of offences related to pawning—itself central to the alternative economy of the poor—women even outstripped the performance of men. From the influential late Victorian historian Luke Owen Pike[41] through to 1930s criminologist Otto Pollack[42] and well beyond, the feared association of growing female autonomy with female deviance has continued, apparently impervious to the actual patterns of recorded crime, which show no changes in levels of female criminality proportionate to the significant changes in women's social, political, legal and economic position across the 20th Century. Again, this is a persistent myth which finds expression in the world of literary fiction, in which intelligent and active figures like Moll Flanders and Becky Sharp, who assert their independence, also exemplify female transgression.

In terms of the argument of the last chapter, what we see here, in other words, is increasing polarisation between those able and unable to establish respectability, with a small minority of women reaching a 'tipping point' which renders them especially vulnerable to criminalisation. In a further dynamic which also fed into the persistence of evaluations of 'character' as a basis for assessing culpability, Zedner argues that the intense stigmatisation of women offenders caused particular damage to their ability to reintegrate in the economy; hence once their 'character' was lost, their need to reoffend was strong. This was a situation which led to a core of habitual female offenders by the end of the century, at which point women represented a striking 61% of those convicted twenty times or more.[43] This figure lends further weight to the polarisation argument: if a greater proportion of women than of men were being reconvicted, this implies that the total number of women involved in the criminal process is even smaller than the proportions recorded in relation to each offence suggest.

---

[41] *A History of Crime in England* op. cit.: for discussion, see Zedner op. cit. p. 25.
[42] *The Criminality of Women* (Philadelphia: University of Pennsylvania Press 1950).
[43] Zedner op. cit. pp. 43–5.

While respectable women might expect the sexual code to lead to a degree of leniency in their treatment at the hands of the criminal justice system, this expectation was heavily contingent on the marks of respectability and good character.[44]

Women's Crime in the 19th Century Novel: Agency, Character and Wilful Blindness

Even in the late 19th Century, then, there is evidence to suggest that ideas of bad character remained especially significant to the treatment of women. So what are we to make of the ousting of Moll Flanders in the 19th Century realist novel? Female offenders are not, of course, absent from 19th Century literature, though—significantly—their patchy representation tends to consist of infanticide and crimes of passion, committed quite often by 'flat', minor characters occupying the margins of novels. Yet when they do find their way to the centre of the literary stage, the assumptions about their conduct and motivations generate some significant—and perhaps surprising—insights.

We might have expected 19th Century novels to be peopled by female offenders like the luckless Nancy in *Oliver Twist*:[45] a victim of her circumstances, and unable to extricate herself from the mesmerising influence of Bill Sikes even when she has reformed. (Indeed, her moral reformation takes place under the influence of Oliver, and hardly seems the product of her own agency.[46]) Nancy's story does exemplify some of the difficulties of female life in early 19th Century London, evoking the place of prostitution as one of the few avenues open to poor women unable to find a secure footing in respectable society. Also significant from this point of view is *Mary Barton*'s Aunt Esther, in whom Elizabeth Gaskell created a

---

[44] Zedner op. cit. p. 26; her assessment of the degree of leniency accorded to women is more cautious than that advanced by Peter King in relation to the first half of the Century, *Crime and Law in England* op. cit. Chapter 5.

[45] First published 1837–9.

[46] See Lisa Rodensky, *The Crime in Mind* op. cit. Introduction and Chapter 1; see in particular pp. 31–2.

sympathetic yet nonetheless unmistakably moralistic vision of the dangers of female wilfulness and loss of reputation.[47] The beautiful and spirited Esther runs off with a man who fails to marry her. Having lost her character, she is unable to reinsert herself into either family or respectable community, and sinks into a demoralised haze of alcohol and prostitution. Yet even for these most powerless of early Victorian women, a measure of agency remains, as is demonstrated by Esther's efforts to communicate important information to her niece across the barriers erected by her social ostracism. A glimpse of such women's sense of their own agency is eloquently shown by testimony quoted by Judith Walkowitz in her study of prostitution in Victorian society: 'I was a servant gal away down in Birmingham. I got tired of workin' and slavin' to make a living, and getting a ------- bad one at that.... After a bit I went to Coventry...and took up with soldiers as was quartered there. I soon got tired of them. Soldiers is good—soldiers is—to walk with and that, but they don't pay; cos why they ain't got no money; so I says to myself, I'll go to Lunnon and I did. I soon found my level there'.[48]

19th Century novels do, then, give some confirmation of the analysis of female criminalisation as structured, successively, around moralism and a moralised process of pathologisation, mainly trained on sexual deviance such as prostitution and failures of motherhood or feminine propriety such as drunkenness or, most extremely, infanticide. As Josephine McDonagh has shown, by this time child murder—reflecting prevailing cultural anxieties—was regarded as more or less exclusively a female activity. Yet public discourse alternated between analyses blaming degenerate mothers and ones pointing the finger rather at the state: the Malthusian Poor Law of 1834, with its abolition of outdoor relief and consequent consignment of many poor families to the street or workhouse, was explicitly accused of producing infanticide.[49] So even here, the cultural signals were mixed. And in fact many 19th Century female offenders in the tradition of literary realism transmit a complex and ambivalent message about women's autonomy.

---

[47]   *Mary Barton* (1848: Penguin Classics 1996).

[48]   Judith R. Walkowitz, *Prostitution and Victorian Society: Women, class and the state* (Cambridge University Press 1980) p. 13.

[49]   *Child Murder and British Culture 1720–1900* op. cit. Chapter 4.

Take, for example, Hetty Sorrell, the respectable farmer's niece loved by George Eliot's *Adam Bede*.[50] Vain and cold-hearted, Hetty's beauty attracts the young local Squire, Arthur Donnithorne. After a confrontation with the wounded Adam, Donnithorne withdraws from the scene, to Hetty's distress: but by this time she is pregnant by him. Concealing her situation from her uncle's family, and, Eliot implies, even from herself, Hetty finally leaves her home in search of Donnithorne. Once she is convinced that she cannot find him, she wanders distractedly until giving birth to the baby, who a short time later is found dead under a pile of leaves. In a fascinating portrait of denial, echoing historical data on the frequency of concealment of birth and pregnancy among infanticides,[51] Hetty asserts her innocence and distances any chance of the exercise of mercy at her trial by her cold and detached demeanour (though she is finally brought to a confession by her cousin, the Methodist Dinah Morris, and is ultimately saved from the scaffold by a reprieve brought by Donnithorne).[52]

Hetty is, certainly, in some sense the victim of male irresponsibility. Indeed, as Rodensky notes, Eliot condemns Arthur, notwithstanding his good intentions, for culpable negligence: Hetty's disaster, and the consequent damage to her family's reputation, to put it in legal terms, being a natural consequence of his seduction of her, he is responsible. But Hetty is also portrayed by George Eliot as the agent of her own misfortune and as bearing a measure of responsibility for her own, and her aunt's and uncle's, fate: her lack of judgment, represented by her vanity and obtuse misreading of her social situation and power over her lover are held up, unmistakably, to the reader's judgment. It is not only her infanticidal act but also her unbridled and unreasonable sexual desire which,

---

[50] (1859: Penguin Classics 1980).

[51] See Mark Jackson (ed.), *Infanticide: historical perspectives on child murder and concealment, 1550–2000* (Ashgate: Aldershot 2002), in particular Johanna Geyer-Kordesch, 'Infanticide and the erotic plot: a feminist reading of eighteenth century crime' pp. 93–127.

[52] Hetty's situation is closely paralleled by another 19th Century literary representation of an infanticide trial: Walter Scott's depiction of the trial of the similarly mute, and yet more misunderstood, Euphemia Deans in *The Heart of Midlothian* (1818: op. cit.); see in particular pp. 224ff. In both novels, the devastating impact on the 'character' of the alleged infanticide's family is emphasised.

as McDonagh puts it, cannot be contained within the new sexual economy, and necessitate her conviction and transportation.[53]

Both Hetty and Arthur, then, are condemned by Eliot for a species of culpable ignorance not dissimilar to the legal concept of 'wilful blindness'. But is Rodensky right to see this notion of objective responsibility as gradually displaced within literary representations in favour of an emerging focus on subjective responsibility? Literary images of responsibility for interior psychological states are certainly not a 19th Century invention. Defoe's *Roxana*, for example, rounds on her faithful servant Amy when the latter admits that she is tempted to kill Susan, the abandoned daughter whose curiosity about her parentage threatens Roxana's social position: 'why you ought to be hang'd for what you have done already; for, having resolv'd on it, is doing it, as to the Guilt of the Fact you are a Murtherer already, as much as if you had done it already'.[54] Rodensky supports her argument that the images of criminality across the 19th Century novels are however becoming increasingly focused on interior states such as intention or desire with a number of examples, several of them drawn from the later novels of George Eliot. One of them is *Felix Holt* (1866), an independent-minded and uncompromising radical who, in a misplaced attempt to mitigate the effects of a riot caused by the machinations of candidates in an election, finds himself charged with encouragement of riot and with a serious assault against a constable. His ultimate exoneration—by not only the novelist but the pardoning process—reveals George Eliot's own view of the moral priority of intentions, and supports Rodensky's thesis about a gradual move to a subjective

[53] *Child Murder and British Culture 1720–1900* op. cit. Chapter 5: note that the novel was written in one era, and set in another, which witnessed considerable public concern about infanticide; moreover Hetty, like Euphemia Deans of *The Heart of Midlothian* (see the previous note) is tried under the draconian 1624 legislation under which concealment of birth produced a presumption of guilt. This legislation was finally abolished in 1803. In a subtle reading of *Adam Bede*, McDonagh argues that in this as in previous generations, a preoccupation with infanticide stood in for broader cultural preoccupations: in the case of Eliot's novel, they include the idea that kindness to children, reflected in both Adam and Dinah, is—like the reform of infanticide law—a mark of progress and civilisation. McDonagh further argues (less persuasively in my view) that child murder in the novel symbolises the forgetting of a violent past on which the nation is founded.

[54] *Roxana* op. cit. p. 273: cf. p. 41 'I was a double Offender, whatever he was; for I was resolv'd to commit the Crime, knowing and owning it to be a Crime; he if it was true as he said, was fully perswaded it was Lawful...'

stance in Eliot's work. In a fascinating glimpse of Judge's world of credibility, and of the intertwining of character and intent, Felix defends himself not only by asserting that the constable 'attacked me under a mistake about my intentions' but also by appealing to 'my own motives, and the testimony that certain witnesses will give to my character and purposes as being inconsistent with my willingly abetting disorder'. As one of the witnesses, Esther Lyon, puts it, in a clear inference from character to intent: 'he could never have had any intention that was not brave and good.'[55] Such is the view of the all-seeing narrator: but in the epistemologically less privileged context of the trial, both eyewitness testimony and Felix's reputation for unconventionality underpin his conviction.

Even here, then, apparently factual judgments of intent are inextricably linked with evaluations of character. Another of Rodensky's examples—Gwendolen Harleth/Grandcourt, one of the two female protagonists of Eliot's *Daniel Deronda* (1876)—illustrates a further reason for resisting the idea of an inexorable turn to purely subjective notions of responsibility.[56] Unhappily married, Gwendolen wishes for the death of her husband. When it ensues, even though it appears that it was the product of an accident, she feels responsible, and suffers a mental collapse. But Gwendolen, like Hetty, though the victim of male selfishness, was previously the author of her own difficulties, having courted the brutal Grandcourt out of the desire to exploit her beauty by marrying into a well-connected

---

[55] *Felix Holt: The Radical* op. cit. pp. 440, 449 and 442 respectively. The book is peppered with references to consciousness, will and intent, and the contrast between Felix's good intentions and the evil consequences of his acts are a central theme.

[56] (Penguin Classics 1995); Rodensky points out that Eliot also explores in *Middlemarch* op. cit. the idea of purely subjective responsibility in relation to Bulstrode, who compasses, and omits to prevent, the death of Raffles. In Bulstrode's case too, however, this ultimate moment of culpable inattention is carefully contextualised within a history of self-deception in which a superstructure of rationalism and religious doctrine allows him to disguise malice and ambition even from himself: 'There may be coarse hypocrites, who consciously affect beliefs and emotions for the sake of gulling the world, but Bulstrode was not one of them. He was simply a man whose desires had been stronger than his theoretic beliefs, and who had gradually explained the gratification of his desires into satisfactory agreement with those beliefs.' p. 667; 'A man vows, and yet will not cast away the means of breaking his vow. Is it that he distinctly means to break it? Not at all; but the desires which tend to break it are at work in him dimly, and make their way into his imagination, and relax his muscles in the very moments when he is telling himself over again the reasons for his vow.' p. 761.

and wealthy family. Though George Eliot flirts with the idea of purely subjective guilt, the real object of her moral assessment lies, with Gwendolen as with Hetty, in self-deception, and in the lack of judgment which produces a wilful blindness to the real state of things. In Eliot's supremely skilled practice of literary realism, to a greater degree than is possible amid the practical imperatives of a criminal trial, responsibility is contextualised within individuals' histories and dispositions, and this, I would argue, conduces to a conceptual framework oriented as much to objective as to subjective notions of responsibility. This is not merely a matter of proof. While external markers of character certainly do serve by this period as indicators of states of mind, principles of responsibility also embrace a conception of fault as grounded in unreasonable character manifested in lack of self-knowledge, poor judgment or self-deception.

The Murderess in the Attic: Derangement, Dissociation and Duality of Mind

As we saw earlier, accounts of 19th Century criminality have often noted the association between female criminality and both sexual deviance and madness. Several of our examples have illustrated the former connection: Esther's, Hetty's, and Tess's offences are all related, in one way or another, to their breach of the norms of sexual propriety and, in Hetty's case, of motherhood. What, however, of the supposed association of women's criminality with madness or mental incapacity? For literary examples, we need to turn to the continuation of the Gothic tradition—to the novel of sensation and to melodrama—which represents a fragmentation of the genre of literary fiction itself reflecting notions of 'high' and 'low' culture which deserve much more attention than I can give them here.[57] Among novels of sensation, a good

---

[57] *Felix Holt* and *Mary Barton* provide good examples of Jan-Melissa Schramm's argument that literary realism in the 19th Century becomes preoccupied with instances of false accusation, reflecting the ascendancy of legal representation for the defence following the Prisoners' Counsel Act 1836; *Testimony and Advocacy in Victorian Law, Literature and Theology* op. cit. Chapter 3; conversely, the books

example for our purposes is Mary Elizabeth Braddon's *Lady Audley's Secret*, published in 1862.[58] Prompted by circumstances of economic distress, the eponymous heroine has assumed a new identity after abandoning her first husband and their child. Married to another man, she is terrified of discovery when her first husband reappears. Her response is to try to kill him by pushing him down a well. After an unsuccessful attempt to kill his friend, who has discovered the truth, she confesses the crime and, declaring that she is mad, reveals her true identity to her second husband. She is finally consigned to a Belgian asylum under yet another assumed identity, so as to avoid shaming the family name.[59] The anxieties displayed here about the difficulty of recognising people—assessing their credibility and character—in a mobile world, and about violations of female domestic, wifely and maternal duty, are both evident, and shared within the realist literary tradition. But in the latter, the madwoman, criminal or otherwise, is conspicuous by her marginality: she tends to be, like *Jane Eyre*'s Bertha Mason (1847), in the attic,[60] or like *Middlemarch*'s Laure (1871–2), at a safe distance (in the past, and, like Lady Audley, in continental Europe).[61] And in the novels of sensation in which women like Lydia Gwilt of Wilkie Collins' *Armadale*—a strikingly Moll-like figure—occupy centre stage,

which I discuss in this paragraph and in note 59 illustrate her contention that the exploration of deviance became focused onto melodrama and sensation novels. As in the case of the Gothic strand in the fictional genre mentioned in Chapter II, however, the fragmentation is not a neat one, with writers like Dickens, for example in *Barnaby Rudge* (1841) or *Bleak House* (1853), and Collins, for example in *The Moonstone* (1868) or *Armadale* (1866), treating both deviance and false accusation, and exhibiting features of both sensationalism and realism. Charlotte Brontë, too, falls into this hybrid category, with *Jane Eyre* (1847: Penguin Classics 2003) displaying unmistakably Gothic touches, notably in the shady presence of Bertha Mason.

[58] (Ware: Wordsworth Classics 1997).

[59] Comparable examples are to be found in the late 18th Century Gothic novels. For example, in Ann Radcliffe's *The Mysteries of Udolpho* (1792: op. cit.) the deranged nun Sister Agnes is finally revealed to be Signora Laurentini, an Italian noblewoman driven to madness by the guilt she feels at having incited her lover, from motives of sexual jealousy, to kill his wife. Possibly one of the first 'madwomen in the attic' (or, as in this case the cloister), Signora Laurentini's story, though crucial to the plot, is only revealed in the last 30 pages of a 650-page novel.

[60] Op. cit.

[61] France in particular seems to have held a special place in novelists' imagination of female crime: Dickens' murderess Hortense in *Bleak House*, like Eliot's Laure, is French. This perhaps relates to the English association of the French revolution with policies conducive to female degeneracy: see Chapter II note 87.

we see a strong orientation to condemnation and punishment, as well as hints of mental instability peculiar to the Victorian imagination.[62]

Female offenders in literary realism do, however, often exemplify a form of mental incapacity which is closely related to self-deception: absence of mind or multiple consciousness. In a fascinating study, Joel Peter Eigen has examined the emergence in the latter part of the 19th Century of a related set of problematic instances of 'unconscious crime' which did not fall squarely within the McNaghten rules' definition of insanity as founded in cognitive failures rooted in the physicalist conception of 'disease of the mind'. These, rather, were failures of volition or of suspended consciousness, often unrelated to disease.[63] Like Rodensky and many other commentators, Eigen's starting point is the assumption that the Victorian focus on self-mastery of the will as the foundation of criminal justice governance implied that knowledge and consciousness were central to criminal responsibility. He further argues that this conception of responsibility took off from a Lockean notion of the unified self: of the criminal law subject as present to, and capable of being known by, itself. Hence the very criminal justice project, with its moralised conception of responsibility, was threatened by this cluster of cases of absent or multiple consciousness.[64]

[62] I have no proof that Lydia was inspired by *Moll Flanders*, but the analogies are striking: not only is she a beautiful, resourceful and property-seeking offender, but she is also assisted to some extent by an older woman—Mother Oldershaw—who bears strong resemblance to Moll's 'governess'. On the other hand, Lydia, unlike Moll, is able to contemplate murder with equanimity; she is also, like her near-contemporary Becky Sharp of *Vanity Fair*, conspicuously vicious towards other women; and, in a distinctively Victorian touch, Collins casts her as a laudanum addict.

[63] *Unconscious Crime: Mental Absence and Criminal Responsibility in Victorian London* (Johns Hopkins University Press 2003).

[64] On the 19th Century history of multiple personality and associated phenomena such as somnambulism as both social preoccupation and object of medical interest, see Ian Hacking, *Rewriting the Soul* op. cit. Chapters 9–14. Significantly for my argument, Hacking locates the professional analysis at mid-century firmly within physicalist, though moralised, notions of illness, notably hysteria and disorders of the nervous system: and he contends that memory as such became an object of scientific interest only towards the end of the century. This happened later in Britain or America than in France, where by 1875 it was already a conceptual truth that 'It was part of the nature of a doubled personality to be a hysteric. It was part of her nature to be hypnotisable. And it was part of her nature to have a *maladie de mémoire*' (p. 170). The ultimate upshot of the development of 'sciences of memory' was that 'what would previously have been debates on the moral and spiritual plane took place at the level of factual knowledge.' (p. 198). Hence Hacking diagnoses another move from evaluation to factualisation, and

It was perhaps the very threat which such dissociated states posed
to their notions of social control which underpinned Victorians'
fascination with these phenomena—a fascination which Eigen
nicely compares to the attitude of someone who is afraid of snakes
but cannot resist visiting the reptile house at the zoo. Focusing
on instances of automatism, sleepwalking, epilepsy, delirium,
irresistible impulses, voices, unconsciousness, loss of memory, or
'deranged morals', Eigen constructs a series of case studies drawn
from the Old Bailey. He finds that, though lying outside the formal
legal definition of insanity, medical testimony was often sought in
these cases, and that juries not infrequently went beyond or behind
the M. Naghten rules to bring in verdicts such as 'not guilty on
grounds of unconsciousness'.[65]

The 19th Century novels certainly reflect this preoccupation with
unconscious or distracted states in their portrayal of female crime,
which often takes place between the interstices of chapters, outside
the reader's line of vision—perhaps symbolising the unspeakable
nature of female violence by this period.[66] Hetty's distraction before
the death of her baby renders it possible that she has instinctively
covered the baby with leaves to hide and protect it, rather than
with a conscious intent to kill it: Gwendolen's psychological state is
such as to make it unclear, even to her, whether she had acted upon
her wish that Grandcourt die by either pushing him from the boat
or, by omission, failing to rescue him. In the words which Hardy
puts in Angel Clare's mouth in relation to Tess just before she kills
Alec, she 'had spiritually ceased to recognise the body before him
as hers—allowing it to drift, like a corpse upon the current, in a
direction dissociated from its living will.'[67] But the Victorian preoccupation with states of absence or duality of mind also applies to
men. Its most famous literary expression is, after all, Robert Louis
Stevenson's *Dr. Jekyll and Mr. Hyde* (1887).[68] *Tess of the d'Urbervilles*,
too, features an extended sleepwalking scene of which Angel Clare
is the subject, while the plot of Wilkie Collins' *The Moonstone*

one which happens at the end rather than the beginning or middle of the 19th
Century.
[65] See Elizabeth Carr's case, Old Bailey Sessions Papers 1875–6 Case 413.
[66] Even Lydia Gwilt's one completed crime takes place before the narrative
begins, and remains shrouded in opaque allusion (*Armadale* op. cit).
[67] *Tess of the d'Urbervilles* op. cit. pp. 394–5.
[68] (New York: Signet Classics 2003).

(1868) is entirely shaped around a 'theft' whose (male) perpetrator turns out to have committed it unconsciously during a state of somnambulism created by laudanum. And this literary evidence is confirmed by the history of medical sciences: while mid-century treatises, predictably, associated female double consciousness with the menstrual cycle, they were concerned with men, too. In his study of the history of multiple personality, Ian Hacking cites one physician in 1836 describing such cases as having 'mostly occurred in young females in whom the uterine functions were disturbed or, if in the male sex, where the nervous system has been weakened by excesses, terror or other cerebral excitement.'[69] (Interestingly, Hacking traces significant differences between French and German constructions of double or multiple personality and British and American ones: in the latter, the preoccupation with such states appears to have connected importantly with the rise not only of particular medical theories but of spiritualism, and, in an amusing parallel, the eclipse of multiple personality coincides with the triumph of psychoanalysis.[70])

Certainly, there is in the novels of both realist and other traditions a sense of the multiplicity of the human mind: as George Eliot puts it in relation to Mrs. Transome, whose complaint about the futility of woman's will framed the last chapter; 'She had never seen behind the canvass with which her life was hung'.[71] And this would have been troubling both to the idea of criminal responsibility as founded in a unitary subject present to itself, and to the accompanying idea that inner states of the human mind are knowable to criminal courts. If we are not transparent to ourselves, what hope, after all, does the criminal trial have of judging our intentions and beliefs? But this perplexity was not and is not specific to female offenders. By the end of the 19th Century, determinist theories had become an important way in which the criminality of both men and women was understood. Beyond this, the institutional mechanisms for evaluating the states of mind

[69] *Rewriting the Soul* op. cit. p. 151.

[70] Ibid, pp. 134–6. Hacking's observation about the links between spiritualism and multiple personality in Britain and America itself finds literary confirmation: for example, *The Moonstone* op. cit. displays an intermittent preoccupation with mesmerism.

[71] *Felix Holt* op. cit. p. 379; cf. the passages on Bulstrode's self-deception quoted in note 56.

of individuals whose psychologies were apprehended as at once increasingly important and increasingly complex were still in the process of development. And the determinist theories, as is reflected in the novels, were as much concerned with social and economic as with dispositional bases of crime: even the supposedly insane Lady Audley, after all, cites what seems to be a perfectly rational, if somewhat exaggerated, reaction to economic duress as the original cause of her behaviour, while in *Barnaby Rudge* (1841) Dickens ponders the relationship between heredity and adverse environment in producing criminal pathology.

Recovering Women's Agency: From Criminality to Unconventionality

It seems, then, that neither the rare examples of female offenders in 19th Century literature, nor their cousins in the criminal courts, are necessarily being treated consistently as 'the weaker half of the human family'. Clearly, notions of women as less fully agents than men did circulate in Victorian ideology, and shaped in particular women's position in family and property law: as is evoked in the title of Frances Power Cobbe's 1868 essay 'Criminals, Idiots, Women and Minors: Is the Classification Sound?'[72] For, though the novels bombard their readers with fascinating data on assumptions about women and their social position and capacity, most of the women in novels from Moll to Tess are recognisable agents with fully fledged rational capacities. Even Tess, who commits the closest thing to a 'crime of passion', is portrayed across much of Hardy's novel as acting autonomously, albeit in a highly constraining world: she is the victim of male cruelty and of her circumstances, but she is also a wilful person. Though Hardy occasionally deploys late Victorian stereotypes of objectified femininity ('A field-man is a personality afield; a field-woman is a portion of the field; she has somehow lost her own margin'[73]), he also gives us

---

[72] *Frazer's Magazine*; reproduced in Susan Hamilton (ed.), *Criminals, Idiots, Women and Minors: Nineteenth Century Writing by Women on Women* (Peterborough: Broadview Press 1995) p. 108. For further discussion see Kieran Dolin, *A Critical Introduction to Law and Literature* op. cit. Chapter 5.
[73] *Tess of the d'Urbervilles* op. cit. Chapter 14 p. 90.

a vivid account of Tess's mental exertions. Notwithstanding the suggestion of a dissociation of will from body, the reader is left in no real doubt of the intentionality with which she commits the murder which condemns her to the gallows. Similarly, her culpability is conceived in terms of concepts central to late Victorian criminal law: not only were her sins before the murder, as Tess herself reflects, 'not sins of intention, but of inadvertence',[74] but in one letter to Angel, her reproach is that 'You know that I did not intend to wrong you'.[75]

From the very beginning of the genre now known as realism, women in novels are utterly recognisable to the modern reader: they reason about values, consequences, strategies; they worry and feel; they hope and dare; on occasion they defy patriarchal authority even in the face of a clear-eyed analysis of the likely (usually grim...) upshot of doing so. They straddle, with insouciance, all the binaries to one side of which prevailing masculine culture (and some feminist theory) have aspired to confine them. Nor were the Victorians blind to the socially constructed nature of aspects of female 'weakness'. As late as 1848, Thackeray juxtaposes in *Vanity Fair* Amelia's exaggerated female weakness and sensibility with the luminous autonomy and hard-headedness of Becky, as well as threading into the interstices of his novel some reflections on the distorting effects of prevailing discourses of femininity which look both back to the arguments of Mary Wollstonecraft and forward to late 20th Century feminism. Here is Thackeray:

'What do men know about women's martyrdom? We should go mad had we to endure the hundredth part of those daily pains which are meekly borne by many women. Ceaseless slavery meeting with no reward; constant gentleness and kindness met by cruelty as constant; love, labour, patience, watchfulness without even so much as the acknowledgment of a good word; all this, how many of them have to bear in quiet, and appear abroad with cheerful faces as if they felt nothing. Tender slaves that they are, they must needs be hypocrites and weak.'[76]

And here, half a century earlier but in similar vein, is Wollstonecraft:

---

[74] *Tess of the d'Urbervilles* op. cit. Chapter 51.
[75] Ibid, p. 370.
[76] *Vanity Fair* op. cit. pp. 663–4.

'Women are told from their infancy, and taught by the example of their mothers, that a little knowledge of human weakness, justly termed cunning, softness of temper, *outward* obedience, and a scrupulous attention to a puerile kind of propriety, will obtain for them the protection of a man; and should they be beautiful, every thing else is needless, for, at least, twenty years of their lives.... An immoderate fondness for dress, for pleasure, and for sway, are the passions of savages; the passions that occupy those uncivilised beings who have not yet extended the dominion of the mind, or even learned to think with the energy necessary to concatenate that abstract train of thought which produces principles. And that women from their education and the present state of civilised life, are in the same condition, cannot, I think, be controverted.... That women are at present by ignorance rendered foolish or vicious is, I think, not to be disputed.'[77]

And here, finally, is French feminist Luce Irigaray, writing 150 years later:

'Men are uncivil as a result of too many rights and too few duties, and women as a result of too few rights and too many duties, for which they compensate by impulsiveness and subjectivity without social bounds, in the form of either persistent childish behaviour or maternal authoritarianism extending into the social sphere.'[78]

The parallels in terms of a concern with environment and education which we saw reflected in the novels of Burney, Edgeworth and Austen, and which assert themselves with equal force in the work of George Eliot, speak for themselves.[79]

[77] Mary Wollstonecraft, *A Vindication of the Rights of Woman* (1792: Penguin Classics edition 2004) pp. 28, 234, 240.

[78] See Luce Irigaray, *Thinking the Difference* (London: Athlone Press 1994) p. 78; see also her comment on p. 82 about women's lack of public responsibilities leaving us (perhaps significantly, she says 'them') 'mired in instability, dissatisfaction, criticism.'

[79] As discussed in the last chapter, however, Wollstonecraft's position on the distorting impact of the culture of sensibility went hand in hand with a strong assertion of women's right to express their feelings, articulated most vividly in her unfinished novel (*Maria* op. cit). This tension between the assertion of women's reason and the impulse to self-expression surface again, and are brought to an interesting, if uncomfortable, synthesis, in the figure of Lucy Snowe in Charlotte Brontë's *Villette* (1853: Penguin Classics 2004): '"But if I feel, may I *never* express?" "*Never!*" declared Reason. I groaned under her bitter sternness. Never—never—oh, hard word! This hag, this Reason, would not let me look up, or smile, or hope: she could not rest unless I were altogether crushed, cowed, broken-in, and broken-down. According to her, I was born only to work for a piece of bread, to await the pains of death, and steadily through all life to despond.

Hetty's and Tess's criminality are, of course, entirely different from that of Moll Flanders. Powerful emotions are portrayed as the source of Hetty's and Tess's offences. They act in worlds which are particularly unforgiving of conduct which transgresses the boundaries not only of law but of conventional femininity. While infanticide often commanded sympathy from all-male juries, Hetty's lack of confession and apparent lack of remorse condemn her, just as Tess's pride and unwillingness to ask for help seal her fate.[80] Yet while both of them lack experience and wisdom, neither Hetty nor Tess lacks rationality or agency: rather, they are prevented by prevailing social norms from exercising that agency in self-determining ways.[81] Their decisive punishment underlines both the state's determination to enforce legal norms and society's condemnation of their violation of the ultimate image of Victorian femininity: care of children, sexual reserve and physical docility.

But given the dearth of female offenders in realist literature, and the projection of female deviance onto less spectacular and more exquisite breaches of social norms, we need to look further afield for evidence of what the Victorians thought about female transgression. If, as Gladfelder has argued, one of the pleasures of the novel under modern conditions has been its representation of transgressions prohibited within increasingly disciplined social life, it may be useful to look beyond literary representations of female criminality to broader representations of female deviance. Here I want to take two examples: William Makepeace Thackeray's Becky

Reason might be right; yet no wonder we are glad at times to defy her, to rush from under her rod and give a truant hour to Imagination—*her* soft, bright foe; *our* sweet Help, our divine Hope. We shall and must break bounds at intervals, despite the terrible revenge that awaits our return.' (pp. 255–6: emphasis in the original). Note Brontë's ironic feminisation of Reason. No wonder Brontë was still struggling with this problem. Her friend and biographer Elizabeth Gaskell, in her portrait of the female-dominated society of *Cranford* (1853: Oxford World's Classics 1998), colours her affectionate sketch with a tinge of rationalist, urban condescension, while giving us, in Miss Mattie, a vivid picture of the costs of an over-developed capacity for self-command and self-denial.

[80] Cf. Wiener, *Men of Blood* op. cit. Chapter 4, on the intense focus on the apparent state of mind of female defendants at trial during this period.

[81] It might be argued that one of the weaknesses of *Tess* is the way in which Hardy almost suspends her agency at crucial turning points in the plot. Compared with her otherwise strong and spirited personality—and even in the light of her sense of responsibility or difficult circumstances—her cession at key moments to her parents', to Angel's, and—most disastrously—to Alec's will seem hard to understand.

Sharp of *Vanity Fair* (1848)[82] and George Eliot's Dorothea Brooke of *Middlemarch* (1871–2):[83] probably the two most luminously intelligent heroines of the 19th Century, and each of them transgressive, albeit in interestingly different ways.[84]

First, let us renew our acquaintance with Becky Sharp—one of Moll Flanders' very few close literary relatives, and as vivid a portrait of early 19th as Moll is of late 17th Century female agency. A clever orphan who seems destined to spend her life as a governess, Becky uses her beauty and talent to expand her social networks, ruthlessly trampling over anyone who gets in the way of her supreme ambition: marriage with a man of status, large wealth, universal admiration, and regular excitement. Having achieved the first, to the detriment of the second, she relies on her talents in securing the third to sustain her position, engaging in outrageous financial exploitation and a dangerous, though initially profitable, extra-marital *liaison*. Like Moll, Becky has a thoroughly capitalist view of the world, implying a subversive connection between money and character: as she memorably puts it to herself, 'I think

---

[82] *Vanity Fair* op. cit. I should acknowledge here that there is some debate about whether *Vanity Fair* counts as an unambiguous part of the realist tradition. The book, after all, echoes many of the preoccupations of the 'Newgate Novels' by authors such as Harrison Ainsworth. As I have already observed, the boundaries between different sub-genres of literary fiction, like those between 'high' and 'low' culture, are highly porous. My judgment is that *Vanity Fair* shows sufficient marks of the realist tradition that it bears comparison with *Middlemarch*. However, the analogies between Becky Sharp and her 'sensation' cousin Lydia Gwilt of *Armadale*—certainly the most gifted unambiguously criminal heroine of Victorian literature—should be noted. In particular, and in contrast to Moll Flanders, the two share a special malice towards other women, an unsuccessful struggle for respectability, and ultimate ostracism. I am grateful to Jan-Melissa Schramm for discussion of this issue.

[83] *Middlemarch*, (1871–2: Penguin Classics, based on the second edition of 1874, 1994).

[84] These are, of course, just two examples from a possible sample of many dozens of strong-willed, enterprising and unconventional women in Victorian literature. What almost all of them share is the experience of unhappiness, frustration and disappointment. From Eliot, I could equally have chosen Maggie Tulliver (*The Mill on the Floss* (1860: Penguin Classics 2003)) or Gwendolen Grandcourt from *Daniel Deronda*, whom we have already encountered. See, beyond other instances already discussed, Mrs (Margaret) Oliphant, *Hester* (1883: London: Virago Modern Classics 1984); Wilkie Collins, *No Name* (1862: Oxford World's Classics 1998). In a rare exception (though one which includes its fair representation of female adversity), Collins has to be credited with the invention of the first female detective: Wilkie Collins, *The Law and the Lady* (1875: Oxford World's Classics 1999).

I could be a good woman if I had five thousand a year. I could dawdle about in the nursery, and count the apricots on the wall.... I could ask old women about their rheumatisms, and order half-a-crown's worth of soup for the poor. I shouldn't miss it much out of five thousand a year.... I could pay everybody, if I had but money.' (Equally subversively, Thackeray adds, 'and who knows but Rebecca was right in her speculations—and that it was only a question of money and fortune which made the difference between her and an honest woman?'[85]) But, unlike Moll, Becky never reforms—nor is she formally punished. (Indeed, though her imaginative manipulations of social convention form an important focus of the narrative, her most egregious breaches of sexual decency and her actual offences—like the implication that she may have murdered her wealthy, vain and gullible companion Joseph Sedley—are hinted at rather than shown, leaving open the interpretation that she is in part a victim of the malicious gossip endemic to the culture of reputation). But she is kept outside respectable society and, eventually, out of England: her wit and guile enable her to find financial stability but not the place in the social order which she craves. It is not Becky's agency or resourcefulness which are punished: rather, it is her malice, selfishness and ruthlessness. Her amorality and perhaps, above all, in the ultimate early Victorian female sin, her lack of maternal feeling, are what finally exile her from polite society. (It is interesting that, even in the relatively mobile Regency world, Thackeray plausibly portrays Becky's bad reputation as following her across the channel to the continent.)

Dorothea Brooke, heroine of George Eliot's most fully realised realist novel, is also an orphan. Far more fortunate than Becky, she and her placid sister Celia are brought up by their genial though ill-judging uncle Mr. Brooke. From the very beginning, it is clear that Dorothea has ambition—Eliot uses the word ardour, which marks the way in which Dorothea's aspirations are at once earnest and non-instrumental—to make something important of her life. Sadly, her opportunities are limited, and her inexperience combines with her enthusiasm to underpin a fatal decision: she projects her ardour onto the elderly cleric and scholar Mr. Casaubon, in whom the trappings of learning and moral seriousness mislead her into thinking him a worthy object of her adoration. Married to

---

[85]   *Vanity Fair* op. cit. Chapter 41 p. 490.

Casaubon, Dorothea's intelligent discernment quickly discovers his superficiality, vanity and fragility. Deeply unhappy, she nonetheless plays the role of the loyal wife, while finding small outlets for her imagination and generous intelligence: in acts of friendship to the equally ambitious and yet more ill-judging Dr. Lydgate; and in an increasingly affectionate interest in Mr. Casaubon's ward, Will Ladislaw. On Casaubon's premature death, Dorothea is released from the narrow servitude of marriage to a man incapable of appreciating her spirit or her judgment. But, despite her wealth and education, her ambitions are circumscribed by the world she lives in, and the best that George Eliot can do for her luminous heroine is to insert her, through an act of self-assertion which itself attracts significant social opprobrium,[86] into a happier marriage with the relatively thinly sketched Ladislaw.

In terms of psychological disposition and moral character, Dorothea and Becky could hardly be more different. But in terms of agency and independence of mind, they bear a strong resemblance. How did George Eliot—the most philosophically sophisticated of 19th Century novelists, and the one most overtly committed to the aspirations of realism—see the gender of her heroine as affecting her fate? The weight of the references to femininity/masculinity in *Middlemarch* make it clear that Eliot saw sex/gender as—to a significant extent—a social construct, albeit a social construct which brought with it a distinctive reality of femininity and masculinity, in two main respects. First, Eliot sees gender difference as producing a particular psychological outlook and ethical stance for women and men; second, she sees it as articulated with a division of labour and social spheres.[87]

In terms of psychological and ethical outlook, the prevailing gender regime is a social construct which in Eliot's view has a number of malign effects, notably on women: in damaging their capacity for self-esteem, in causing unhappiness by alienating them from satisfying work; and in encouraging superficiality, vanity and egoism. In terms which evoke the words of Thackeray and Wollstonecraft quoted above, she comments on Rosamond; 'She was oppressed by ennui, and by that dissatisfaction which in

---

[86] Because Casaubon's will expresses his distrust of her by disinheriting her should she remarry.

[87] See *Middlemarch* op. cit. pp. 72, 424–5, 120, 387, 253, 410, 474–5, 647, 431.

women's minds is continually turning into a trivial jealousy refer-
ring to no real claims, springing from no deeper passion than the
vague exactingness of egoism, and yet capable of impelling action
as well as speech.'[88] But the gender regime also had an adverse
impact on men—in obstructing self-knowledge and encouraging
pomposity and self-deceiving rationalisation;[89] and on the social
order, through women's capacities to contribute being blocked.[90]
Admittedly, Eliot often puts stereotypes of femininity into the
mouths of her (usually male) characters[91] in such a way as to make
them seem foolish, particularly in their association of womanly virtue with appearance, submission and seductiveness. But this does
not obstruct her serious analysis of the power of gendered assumptions. Albeit as a result of social forces, women and men have in
her view certain core capacities and sensibilities which conjure up
a distinctive ethic (as well as distinctive moral deformations akin

[88] Ibid, p. 647; see also pp. 474–5, 810. See for example Dorothea's tendency
for self-sacrifice and exaggerated sense of duty, as well as the way in which her
position as a woman leads others—Brooke, Casaubon, Chettam—to obstruct
her self-determination and to some extent her capacity for moral development
(p. 790). Further malign effects of conventional gender assumptions held up to
critical scrutiny in the novel include their impact on women's capacity for self-
esteem (Mrs Garth's preference for male children and its impact on Mary and
Letty); the boredom and unhappiness that women's alienation from work or, in
the case of less privileged women, from satisfying careers, entails (Dorothea pp.
790, 424–5), as well as the vanity, jealousy, gossip that enforced leisure breeds in
women (pp. 798, 647, 115–7). Significantly, none of the three principal female
characters become mothers—a primary source of socially valued female occupation—during the main course of the novel, allowing Eliot to concentrate both
on gender relations unmediated by shared parenthood, while accentuating the
anomie—in both Rosamond's and Dorothea's very different cases—which can
come from lack of meaningful occupation.

[89] See for example Lydgate's (ibid, pp. 120, 387) and Casaubon's (pp. 312–2,
410) unrealistic, infantile conception of marriage and what it can deliver; Mr.
Brooke's lack of self-knowledge and pomposity (pp. 424–5); Bulstrode's capacity
for self-deceiving rationalisation through 'theory' (pp. 565, 667); Lydgate's temptation to 'generalise' about women (p. 632); the male Middlemarch chorus's pomposity and self-importance (pp. 115–17).

[90] In these respects siblings Rosamond and Fred Vincy are a particularly interesting example in that, though they share the same pampered upbringing, Fred
manages to escape it, to do 'moral travel' (see Victoria McGeer, 'Moral travel
and the narrative work of forgiveness', paper on file with the author), while
Rosamond does not. Though brother and sister both secure the affection of part-
ners notably more sagacious than them, the fact that Fred is a man, expected to
pay his way and make his mark, helps to provide a motivation to grow up and
achieve independence which Rosamond's female condition obstructs.

[91] See for example in relation to Lydgate (ibid, pp. 120, 387, 391, 632, 638,
793). Chettam (p. 790), Brooke (pp. 424–5, 790), Casaubon (pp. 312–3, 410).

to those voiced by Thackeray, Wollstonecraft and Irigaray): gender affects both women's opportunities and their powers of judgment.

Dorothea's gender, therefore, shapes her capacity for living an autonomous life. But, as her ardent ambition to make her mark on the world attests, it does not deprive her of agentic capacity to form aspirations and to take responsibility for her own decisions, life and even 'character'. Eliot's view of character is subtle and many-faceted. While character is indeed 'a process and an unfolding',[92] 'not cut in marble', it is also strongly related to dispositions and capacities for which we are not really responsible (in the sense that there are real limits to our capacity as agents fundamentally to change these basic dispositions.)[93] Consequently Eliot holds up as uncivilised the idea of people being condemned by a received view of their character, in a passage which gives some credence to Rodensky's thesis about the move to subjective principles of judgment. As she puts it in Lydgate's voice: 'It is still possible that Bulstrode was innocent of any criminal intention—even possible that he had nothing to do with the disobedience, and merely abstained from mentioning it. But all that has nothing to do with the public belief. It is one of those cases on which a man is condemned on the ground of his character—it is believed he has committed a crime in some undefined way, because he had the motive for doing it; and Bulstrode's character has enveloped me, because I took his money. I am simply blighted—like damaged ear of corn...'[94]

On one level, Eliot presents a vision of character as shaped by environment and opportunity, where the power of socialisation and education is repeatedly asserted. But an equally strong theme reflects the early Victorian notion—equally present in the very different utilitarian and evangelical traditions—of our being in some sense responsible for our characters: of character as shapeable by human will. And this multi-faceted social theory which underlies

---

[92] Ibid, p. 178; cf. '"Would you not like to be the one person who believed in that man's innocence, if the rest of the world belied him? Besides there is a man's character beforehand to speak for him." "But my dear Mrs Casaubon," said Mr Farebrother, smiling gently at her ardour, "character is not cut in marble,—it is not something solid and unalterable. It is something living and changing, and may become diseased as our bodies do."' (ibid, p. 790).

[93] This dispositional view of character is used at the start of the novel, explicitly, to explain Dorothea's and Celia's very different adaptation to their circumstances.

[94] Ibid, p. 821.

the book has significant implications for Eliot's conceptions of both female agency and human responsibility and its limits: Dorothea is George Eliot's heroine not only because of her ardour but also because of her conscious struggle to reconcile her objective situation with her aspirations.

Her objective situation is, however, that of an intelligent woman born into a world which Eliot sees as marked by normative assumptions about sexually separate spheres. Significant here is Eliot's sense of the decisive impact of marriage on women's lives, and of the interaction between gender, money and social class. While for several of the male characters, money is a way out of (or lack of money a way into) decisive social constraints,[95] for women, though money is an important factor, it is impossible to buy (or work) their way out of their gender position. They can, of course, marry out of their class position,[96] and an extended, critical meditation on marriage—its gender dynamics and its limits and strengths as a way of life—is one of the centrepieces of the novel.[97] Women's marital choices structure their public reputation. And in each of her marital choices, Dorothea breaches conventional norms in an effort at self-assertion: first, she marries the manifestly unsuitable, elderly, selfish Casaubon; second, she flouts norms of both patriarchy and property by ignoring Casaubon's testamentary injunction and marrying Ladislaw. As Eliot puts it, 'Those who had not seen anything of Dorothea usually observed that she could not have been 'a nice woman', else she would not have married either the one or the other. Certainly those determining acts of her life were not ideally beautiful. They were the mixed result of a young and noble impulse struggling amidst the conditions of an imperfect social state...For there is no creature whose inward being is so strong that it is not greatly determined by what lies outside it.'[98]

Equally, marriage implies a surrender of autonomy and a submission to a division of labour. As Celia puts it,

'"Now, Dodo, do listen to what James [Celia's husband] says...else you will be getting into a scrape. You always did, and you always will, when you set about doing as you please. And I think it is a mercy now after

---

[95] This is true in different ways for Bulstrode, Lydgate and Fred Vincy.

[96] As both Rosamond and Mrs Bulstrode do.

[97] In her analysis of the marriages of the Lydgates, the Garths, the Bulstrodes, the Casaubons, the Chettams, the Vincys, the Cadwalladers.

[98] Ibid, p. 838.

all that you have got James to think for you. He lets you have your plans, only he hinders you from being taken in. And that is the good of having a brother instead of a husband. A husband would not let you have your plans."

"As if I wanted a husband!" said Dorothea. "I only want not to have my feelings checked at every turn." Mrs Casaubon was still undisciplined enough to burst into angry tears.

"...You used to submit to Mr Casaubon quite shamefully...."

"Of course I submitted to him, because it was my duty; it was my feeling for him..."

"Then why can't you think it your duty to submit a little to what James wishes?....Because he only wishes what is for your own good. And, of course men know best about everything, except what women know better....I mean about babies and those things." [99]

Despite the gentle sarcasm, it is clear that Eliot sees an irreducible tension here, and one which perhaps helps to explain the book's unsatisfactory ending. The prevailing shape of gender in the social world Eliot is writing about means that there is simply no space, within the parameters of the realism of which she was the pre-eminent literary practitioner, to let Dorothea's character develop fully, even once she is liberated from her self-imposed servitude to Casaubon. Hence she is married off to Ladislaw, the least fully developed of the principal characters, and the novel ends abruptly— relieving Eliot of the impossible task of showing us how Dorothea's distinctive virtues and aspirations could ever be fully realised in the early Victorian world. (It is instructive in this context to reflect on the fact that *Middlemarch*, like several of George Eliot's other novels, is punctuated by comparisons—sometimes ironic, but with

[99] Ibid, p. 790; Cf. Lydgate: 'He took a wife.... to adorn the remaining quadrant of his course, and be a little moon that would cause hardly a calculable perturbation....To a man under such circumstances, taking a wife is something more than a question of adornment, however highly he may rate this; and Lydgate was disposed to give it the first place among wifely functions. To his taste, guided by a single conversation, this was where Miss Brooke would be found wanting, notwithstanding her undeniable beauty. She did not look at things from the proper feminine angle. The society of such women was about as relaxing as going from your work to teach the second form, instead of reclining in a paradise with sweet laughs for bird-notes, and blue eyes for a heaven.' (p. 120); 'Lydgate relied much on the psychological difference between what for the sake of variety I will call goose and gander: especially on the innate submissiveness of the goose as beautifully corresponding to the strength of the gander.' (p. 391).

a vein of seriousness—between the period which she is writing about and the more 'civilised' world of the audience for whom she is writing.) Perhaps the fact that Ladislaw is such an elusive, under-drawn character serves to muffle the questions with which any thoughtful reader of *Middlemarch* is left: because we don't really know him, we are relieved of the burden of imagining his and Dorothea's life together. In a real sense—a sense which exceeds the closure entailed by the mere ending of the book, and indeed before that ending—Dorothea, the supreme creation of George Eliot's literary imagination, simply disappears.[100] Precisely because of her commitment to realism, and in a striking metaphor for the dual thinkability and yet lived impossibility of female agency in the 19th Century, Eliot, the creator of three of the most luminously agentic female figures in Victorian literature—Dorothea, Gwendolen, and Maggie Tulliver from *The Mill on the Floss* (1860)—buries each of them in, respectively, an unbelievable marriage, an unbearable marriage, and a premature death.

The Disembedding of 'Character': The Fate of Moll at the Hands of Money, Manners, Morals and Medicine

As befits a book ranging over an unmanageably large—though, I trust, colourful—terrain, the themes which I am able to draw out in this conclusion have several dimensions. Culturally, notions of women's agency, the emergence of psychological individualism, and along with them capacity-based notions of responsibility are emerging even in the early part of the 18th Century. Indeed, they are central to the bourgeois ideals which the genre of the realist novel represents. But this does not entail that they were formed

---

[100] Of course, it would be wrong to suggest that Eliot entirely imprisons her characters in their gendered roles: in Mr. Farebrother's and Caleb Garth's participation in the local, the particular, the affective, the private; in Lydgate's empathy with his patients; in Dorothea's aspirations to do something great, good, noble; in Mary Garth's hard-headed realism and strength of purpose, we see many instances of 'gender-bending'—emphasising the capacity of individuals to cross the boundaries set by the social order. In this as in other matters, Eliot's interpretation is subtle.

precisely as we understand them today, nor that they were the primary driving forces in the criminal process in which—as in the political process—bourgeois interests took well over a century to prevail. As in the older, celebrated case of the attribution of criminal responsibility to animals[101] (a practice which persisted in several parts of Europe right up to the modern period) criminal justice arrangements can—and sometimes need to—draw on patterns of responsibility-attribution which are strikingly different from those predominating in contemporary moral thinking or polite culture. In 18th Century England, ideas about identity and agency were in flux, and practices of criminal responsibility-attribution were still largely operating in terms of information and assumptions about conduct, character and reputation—assumptions which are illuminated by the novels we have considered, and which the particular resources of, and demands upon, the criminal process enabled and dictated. Defective female moral character could underpin the criminalisation of women just as it did that of men; but women's relatively secure position in the agricultural economy of early modern England, along with the vitality of informal social controls in rural areas, kept them a minority of offenders officially proceeded against.

The exception—and the factor which I have argued comes closest to explaining the various records of relatively high levels of female criminality—had to do with urbanisation. This was already a significant phenomenon by the end of the 17th Century, and it posed a challenge to the informal mechanisms of social control which were such an important supplement to formal criminal justice in 18th Century England.[102] This was particularly so for women, for a number of reasons. From the late 17th Century, England saw very significant population flows of women from countryside to urban areas, with cities exhibiting an over-representation of female inhabitants right through to the end of the 19th Century. This gender imbalance was, of course, particularly acute during wartime—another factor which helps to explain the very high levels of recorded female crime in London in the last decades of the 17th and

---

[101] E.P. Evans, *The Criminal Prosecution and Capital Punishment of Animals* (Heinemann 1906, Faber 1987).
[102] See Morgan and Rushton, *Rogues, Thieves and the Rule of Law* op. cit. Chapter 2; Allyson N. May, *The Bar and the Old Bailey 1750–1850* op. cit. pp. 8–9.

first of the 18th Century.[103] Many of these women were single, and they occupied particularly economically vulnerable positions in the unstable early capitalist economy.[104] The difficulty of finding safe and affordable accommodation which was consistent with prevailing norms of female respectability was a particular, and growing, problem for women in terms of presenting evidence of good character. For the distinction between lodging houses and houses of 'ill repute' was notoriously blurred—and lodging houses were the only resort for those not in domestic service or otherwise provided with accommodation by their employers.[105]

As John Beattie has shown, these significant numbers of women like Moll—often independent of men or family structures, hence escaping patriarchal control, and unstably articulated with the economy—became from quite early on a specific object of respectable fears.[106] At the end of the 17th and start of the 18th Century, Beattie has calculated—extrapolating from figures for 1694 and 1704—that 80% of the women tried at the Old Bailey for theft were unmarried. It was anxiety about the danger which these independent and economically insecure women represented which seems likely to have prompted, in 1691, the extension of benefit of clergy to women. This would have removed a significant factor inhibiting the prosecution of women, who were formerly liable to capital punishment for even trivial offences. A little later, common forms of property crime particularly associated with women were, conversely, removed from benefit of clergy (shoplifting in 1699 and thefts by servants in 1713).

As we saw in Chapter II, more general fears about the potentially corrupting effects of urbanisation and commercialisation, vividly reflected in novels, were gradually leading to the development of a set of ideas about a compensating code of polite manners—a conventional public morality which would distinguish the newly emerging middle class. One aspect of this was the culture of sensibility—a culture in which women became in an important sense primary bearers of the marks of civilisation,

---

[103] See Peter King, *Crime and Law in England* op. cit. pp. 212–13; J.M. Beattie, *Policing and Punishment in London* op. cit. pp. 69–71.
[104] See Gareth Stedman Jones, *Outcast London* op. cit. pp. 20–38, 83–88.
[105] See Zedner, *Women, Crime and Custody in Victorian England* op. cit. pp. 64ff; Feeley and Little, 'The Vanishing Female', op. cit.
[106] See J.M. Beattie, *Policing and Punishment in London* op. cit. pp. 64–71.

both in themselves and as those responsible for the propagation of this culture in their roles as the socialisers of children. It is easy to imagine that this emerging, feminised, culture must have exacerbated the problems of independent urban single women like Moll: without, as she repeatedly puts it, 'friends' in polite society,[107] it would have been almost impossible for urban women to find a secure social and economic footing—circumstances which must have increased the temptation to opt, like Moll, for a life of crime. Equally, the perception of uncontrolled and dangerous women as a significant social problem would have increased the willingness to prosecute and punish. Notwithstanding arguments about continuing 'leniency' to women across the 18th Century,[108] Walker's differentiated analysis of the treatment of different forms of crime in 17th Century Cheshire[109] suggests that it would be worth engaging in a similar analysis of female property crime specifically in urban areas.[110] Only on the basis of this kind of research will we be in a position to assess whether the fears about female criminality which surface so clearly in the spectacular Old Bailey figures for 1684–1720 may in fact have persisted, in relation to specific types of urban crime, for a yet longer period. My hunch is that this will indeed turn out to have been the case.

Throughout the period from Moll to Tess, literary sources show clearly that women are fully recognised as human, and increasingly as psychological, agents. Yet they are also recognised as operating within a very specific set of constraints—constraints which are shifting over time. The real problem for women, it seems, is not so much assumed weakness or lack of rational agency, but rather the

---

[107] As Naomi Tadmor has shown, what Moll would have meant by this was not friendship as we understand it today, but rather a network of close acquaintance—based on affective or kinship ties, shared business concerns, or political allegiance—with whom she enjoyed relationships characterised by mutual trust and service: *Family and Friends in Eighteenth-Century England* op. cit. Chapters 5–7: Chapter 7 includes a perceptive analysis of the various nuances of 'friendship' in Samuel Richardson's *Clarissa*.

[108] See Peter King, *Crime and Law in England* op. cit. Chapter 5.

[109] Walker, *Crime, Gender and Social Order* op. cit. Chapter 5; David F. Greenberg's differentiated analysis of Old Bailey data from the 18th and 19th Century also provides evidence of marked variation in levels of female involvement in different categories of even property crime: see 'The Gendering of Crime in Marxist Theory' op. cit. pp. 416–17.

[110] King's (op. cit., see especially p. 195) and Zedner's (op. cit.) analyses of patterns of female offending across the 19th Century would lend weight to this claim.

constraints and expectations associated with femininity in general and with marriage and motherhood in particular. In this respect, it is significant that almost all of the women literary figures we have considered are, in effect, childless, and that many of them are unmarried or, as we might say of Moll and Becky, somewhat loosely attached to the roles of both wife and mother. Here again, there is a historical shift: Moll, who has a remarkable capacity for losing track of her children, without apparent distress, is judged far less harshly than Becky, Hetty or even the understandably ambivalent mother, Tess. By the Victorian era, as George Eliot comments; 'It is a fact perhaps kept a little too much in the background, that mothers have a self larger than their maternity...'[111] Women's role as the cultural bearers of developing markers of polite manners—along with the status involved in a man's economic ability to support a wife at home, in charge of the domestic sphere—fed into a longer-standing image of women as less dangerous than men. But when women's social position took them outside these emerging conventions—because of their poverty or sexual adventurousness, or their presence in urban areas in economically fragile and independent positions—the increasingly organised state quickly became interested in controlling them.

From the early to the late 19th Century, as Zedner has shown, there was certainly a move from treating women as criminally responsible to constructing them as the objects of various new social regulations framed in terms of moralised conceptions of health and public order dressed up in scientific garb: the control of inebriates and prostitution were prominent among these, though both the former, and associated policies like those directed to the 'feeble-minded', did apply to men, too. But up to this point, there is little reason to suppose that the images of agency (equally if not more strongly associated with characters of lower status like Moll and Pamela, or indeed in a much earlier period with Chaucer's doughty Wife of Bath) which are so central to the novels are any less present in the court room. The literary transition from Moll to Tess does, therefore, represent something real: but it is a reality about women's social environment rather than an emerging inability to conceive women as moral agents.

---

[111]   *Felix Holt* op. cit. p. III.

In the slow movement from a world in which criminal judgment is motivated by type- or status-based assessments of culpability, to a world in which individual psychological states become the object of proof in criminal trials—a move which is not, in my view, complete until the mid-20th Century, and which encompasses even today only part of the terrain of criminal law—Moll Flanders stands as a fascinating landmark. The question which she poses—what counts as good character, as being a gentlewoman, in an emerging capitalist world in which the same characteristics are needed for sharp practice and for commercial success—echoes down the centuries since her creation, and has as yet not been satisfactorily answered. In the long search for an answer, Moll's female descendants were caught up for over two centuries in a clutch of normative developments—of manners, morals and, finally, medicine—which contributed to the unthinkability of Moll by the era of Tess. In the mean time, the criminal process was slowly being reshaped so as to project, at least at the level of ideology, the central attribution of responsibility onto factual, psychological states which—once the appropriate institutions had been developed—could be operationalised irrespective of dissent about criteria of evil, wicked conduct or bad character. In the gradual dismantling of a status society, the status of womanhood appears to have been reinforced before becoming—incompletely—one of the last fixed marks of social status to be dissolved. I leave it to my readers to judge whether, in 2008, Moll Flanders is thinkable again—and, if so, whether this is a good thing or a bad.

Bibliography

Novels and Other Works of Fiction

Jane Austen, *Sense and Sensibility* (1811: Penguin Classics 1995)

Jane Austen, *Mansfield Park* (1814: Penguin Classics 1996)

Jane Austen, *Persuasion* (1818: Penguin Classics 1998)

Aphra Behn, *Oroonoko or The Royal Slave, a True History* (1688: Penguin Classics 2003)

Mary Elizabeth Braddon, *Lady Audley's Secret* (1862: Ware: Wordsworth Classics 1997)

Charlotte Brontë, *Jane Eyre* (1847: Penguin Classics 2003)

Charlotte Brontë, *Villette* (1853: Penguin Classics 2004)

Frances Burney, *Evelina or, The History of a Young Lady's Entrance into the World* (1778: Penguin Classics 1994)

Frances Burney, *Cecilia or, Memoirs of an Heiress* (1782: Oxford World's Classics 1999)

Frances Burney, *Camilla or, A Picture of Youth* (1796: Oxford World's Classics 1971)

John Cleland, *Fanny Hill: Memoirs of a Woman of Pleasure* (1749: Ware: Wordsworth Classics 2000)

Wilkie Collins, *No Name* (1862: Oxford World's Classics 1998)

Wilkie Collins, *Armadale* (1866: Penguin Classics 1995)

Wilkie Collins, *The Moonstone* (1868: Oxford World's Classics 1999)

Wilkie Collins, *The Law and the Lady* (1875: Oxford World's Classics 1999)

Charlotte Dacre, *Zofloya or The Moor* (1806: Oxford World's Classics 1997)

Daniel Defoe, *Moll Flanders (The History and Misfortunes of the Famous Moll Flanders)* (1722: Penguin Classics 1989)

Daniel Defoe, *Roxana: The Fortunate Mistress* (1724: Oxford World's Classics 1996)

Charles Dickens, *Oliver Twist* (1837–8: Penguin Classics 2002)

Charles Dickens, *Barnaby Rudge* (1841: Oxford World's Classics 2003)

Charles Dickens, *Bleak House* (1853: Penguin Classics 2003)

Charles Dickens, *A Tale of Two Cities* (1859: Penguin Classics 2000)

Charles Dickens, *Our Mutual Friend* (1865: Penguin Classics 1997)

Maria Edgeworth, *Belinda* (1801: Oxford World's Classics 1994)

George Eliot, *Adam Bede* (1859: Penguin Classics 1985)

George Eliot, *The Mill on the Floss* (1860: Penguin Classics 2003)

George Eliot, *Felix Holt: The Radical* (1866: Penguin Classics 1995)

George Eliot, *Middlemarch* (1871–2: Penguin Classics, based on the 2nd ed of 1874, 1994)

George Eliot, *Daniel Deronda* (1876: Penguin Classics 1995)

Henry Fielding, *An Apology for the Life of Mrs Shamela Andrews* (1741: Penguin Classics 1999)

Henry Fielding, *Joseph Andrews* (1742: Penguin Classics 1999)

Henry Fielding, *Jonathan Wild* (1743: Oxford World's Classics 2003)

Henry Fielding *The History of Tom Jones, A Foundling* (1749: Oxford World's Classics 1996)

Henry Fielding, *Amelia* (1751: Oxford: Clarendon Press 1988)

Sarah Fielding, *The Adventures of David Simple, Containing An Account of His Travels Through the Cities of London and Westminster, In the Search of A Real Friend* (1744: Penguin Classics 2002)

Elizabeth Gaskell, *Cranford* (1853: Oxford World's Classics 1998)

Elizabeth Gaskell, *Mary Barton* (1859: Penguin Classics 1980)

John Gay, *The Beggars' Opera* (1728: Penguin Classics 1986)

William Godwin, *Things as They Are, or, The Adventures of Caleb Williams* (1794: Penguin Classics 1988)

Oliver Goldsmith, *The Vicar of Wakefield* (1766: Oxford World's Classics 1974)

Thomas Hardy, *Tess of the d'Urbervilles* (1891: Bantam Classic 2004)

Mary Hays, *Memoirs of Emma Courtney* (1796: Oxford World's Classics 1996)

Eliza Haywood, *Love in Excess: Or, the Fatal Enquiry* (1719–20: Broadview Literary Texts 2000)

Elizabeth Inchbald, *A Simple Story* (1791: Oxford World's Classics 1988)

Elizabeth Inchbald, *Nature and Art* (1794: Teddington: The Echo Library 2006)

Charlotte Lennox, *The Female Quixote: or, The Adventures of Arabella* (1752: Oxford World's Classics 1989)

Thomas Mackenzie, *The Man of Feeling* (1771: Oxford World's Classics 2001)

Mrs (Margaret) Oliphant, *Hester* (1883: London: Virago Modern Classics 1984)

Alexander Pope, *The Dunciad* (1728–43: London: Longman 1999)

Ann Radcliffe, *The Mysteries of Udolpho* (1792: Penguin Classics 1998)

Samuel Richardson, *Pamela, or, Virtue Rewarded* (1740: Penguin Classics, 1985)

Samuel Richardson, *Clarissa, or, The History of a Young Lady* (1747–8: Riverside Editions 1962)

Walter Scott, *The Heart of Midlothian* (1818: Penguin Classics 1994)

Tobias Smollett, *The Adventures of Roderick Random* (1748: Oxford World's Classics 1979)

Tobias Smollett, *The Expedition of Humphry Clinker* (1771: Oxford World's Classics 1998)

Laurence Sterne, *The Life and Opinions of Tristram Shandy, Gentleman* (1759–67: Oxford World's Classics 1998)

Robert Louis Stevenson, *Dr. Jekyll and Mr. Hyde* (1886: New York: Signet Classics 2003)

Jonathan Swift, *Gulliver's Travels* (1726: Penguin Classics 2001)

Jonathan Swift, *Corinna* (1731)

William Makepeace Thackeray, *Vanity Fair: A Novel Without a Hero* (1848: rev. ed 1851: Penguin Classics 2001)

Mary Wollstonecraft, *Maria, or The Wrongs of Woman* (1798: Dover Publications: Mineola, New York 2005)

Articles, Essays and Monographs

C.J.W. Allen, *The Law of Evidence in Victorian England* (Cambridge University Press 1997)

Richard D. Altick, *The Common Reader: A Social History of the Mass Reading Public 1800–1900* (T. University of Chicago Press 1957)

Donna T. Andrew, *London Debating Societies 1776–1799* (London Record Society 1994) http://www.british-history.ac.uk/source.asp?pubid=238

Donna T. Andrew, 'The press and public apologies in eighteenth-century London', in Norma Landau (ed.), *Law, Crime and English Society* p. 208

Maria Aristodemou, *Law and Literature: Journeys from Her to Eternity* (Oxford University Press 2000)

Mary Astell, *A Serious Proposal to the Ladies* (1694: *Parts I and II* Patricia Springborg (ed.), Ontario: Broadview Literary Texts 2002)

J.H. Baker, *The Law's Two Bodies: Some Evidential Problems in English Legal History* (Oxford: Clarendon Press 2001)

Hannah Barker, 'Women, work and the industrial revolution: female involvement in the English printing trades', in Barker and Chalus (eds.), *Gender in Eighteenth Century England* p. 81

Hannah Barker, *The Business of Women: Female Enterprise and Urban Development in Northern England 1760–1830* (Oxford University Press 2006)

Hannah Barker and Elaine Chalus (eds), *Gender in Eighteenth Century England* (London: Longman 1997)

G.J. Barker-Benfield, *The Culture of Sensibility: Sex and Society in Eighteenth-Century England* (University of Chicago Press 1996)

John M. Beattie, 'The Criminality of Women in Eighteenth Century England' 8 *Journal of Social History* (1975) 80–116

John M. Beattie, *Crime and the Courts in England 1660–1800* (Princeton University Press 1986)

John M. Beattie, 'Scales of Justice' 9 *Law and History Review* (1991) 221

John M. Beattie, *Policing and Punishment in London 1660–1750: Urban Crime and the Limits of Terror* (Oxford University Press 2001)

John Bender, *Imagining the Penitentiary: Fiction and the Architecture of Mind in Eighteenth Century England* (University of Chicago Press 1987)

Jeremy Bentham, *An Introduction to the Principles of Morals and Legislation* H.L.A. Hart and J.H. Burns (eds.) (1781; London: Athlone Press 1970) (2nd ed, Oxford: Clarendon Press, 1996)

Guyora Binder, 'The Rhetoric of Motive and Intent' *Buffalo Criminal Law Review* (2002) 1–96

William Blackstone, *Commentaries on the Laws of England* Vol. IV 1765–9 (University of Chicago Press 1979)

Peter Brooks, *The Melodramatic Imagination* (New York: Columbia University Press 1985)

Peter Brooks, *Troubling Confessions: Speaking Guilt in Law and Literature* (Chicago University Press 2000)

Judith Butler, *Gender Trouble: Feminism and the Subversion of Identity* (New York and London: Routledge 1999)

David J.A. Cairns, *Advocacy and the Making of the English Criminal Trial 1800–1865* (Oxford: Clarendon Press 1998)

W.B. Carnochan, *Confinement and Flight* (Berkeley: University of California Press 1977)

Elaine Chalus, 'That epidemical Madness: women and electoral politics in the late eighteenth century', in Barker and Chalus (eds.), *Gender in Eighteenth Century England* p. 151

Frances Power Cobbe, 'Criminals, Idiots, Women and Minors: Is the Classification Sound?' (1868) *Frazer's Magazine*, reproduced in Susan Hamilton (ed.), *Criminals, Idiots, Women and Minors: Nineteenth Century Writing by Women on Women* (Peterborough: Broadview Press 1995) p. 108

Stefan Collini, *Public Moralists: Political Thought and Intellectual Life in Britain 1850–1930* (Oxford University Press 1991)

Philip Collins, *Dickens and Crime* (2nd ed, London: Macmillan 1965)

Carolyn A. Conley, *The Unwritten Law: Criminal Justice in Victorian Kent* (Oxford University Press 1991)

Richard Connors, 'Poor Women, the parish and the politics of poverty', in Barker and Chalus (eds.), *Gender in Eighteenth Century England* p. 127

Susanna Maria Cooper, *The Exceptional Mother* (1769)

Leonore Davidoff and Catherine Hall, *Family Fortunes: Men and Women of the English Middle Class, 1780–1850* (London: Hutchinson 1987)

Kieran Dolin, *A Critical Introduction to Law and Literature* (Cambridge University Press 2007)

Mary Douglas, *How Institutions Think* (Syracuse: Syracuse University Press 1986)

Markus Dubber and Lindsay Farmer (eds.), *Modern Histories of Crime and Punishment* (Stanford University Press 2007)

Maria Edgeworth, *Letters for Literary Ladies, to which is added, An Essay on the noble science of self-justification* (1795: London: Everyman 1993)

Susan Edwards, *Women on Trial* (Manchester University Press 1984)

Joel Peter Eigen, *Witnessing Insanity: Madness and Mad-Doctors in the English Court* (New Haven: Yale University Press 1995)

Joel Peter Eigen, *Unconscious Crime: Mental Absence and Criminal Responsibility in Victorian London* (Baltimore, Johns Hopkins University Press 2003)

Norbert Elias, *The Civilising Process* (1939: Vols 1–3: New York: Pantheon 1978, 1982 and 1983, respectively)

Doreen Elliot, *Gender, Delinquency and Society* (Aldershot: Avebury 1988)

E.P. Evans, *The Criminal Prosecution and Capital Punishment of Animals* (London: Heinemann 1906; Faber 1987)

Malcolm Feeley, 'The Decline of Women in the Criminal Process: A Comparative History' 15 *Criminal Justice History* (1994) 235–74

Malcolm Feeley and Deborah Little, 'The Vanishing Female: The decline of women in the criminal process 1687–1912' *Law and Society Review* (1981) 719

Henry Fielding, 'Essay on the Knowledge of the Characters of Men' in *Miscellanies* (1743) Vol. 1, Henry Knight Miller (ed.) (Oxford: Clarendon Press, 1972)

Henry Fielding, *An Enquiry in to the Causes of the Late Increase in Robbers* (1751), Malvin R. Zirker (ed.) (Oxford: Clarendon Press 1988)

Margot C. Finn, *The Character of Credit: Personal Debt in English Culture, 1740–1914* (Cambridge University Press 2003)

George P. Fletcher, *Rethinking Criminal Law* (Boston and Toronto: Little Brown 1978)

Richard R. Follett, *Evangelicalism, Penal Theory and the Politics of Criminal Law Reform in England, 1808–30* (Basingstoke: Palgrave 2001)

James Fordyce, *Sermons to Young Women* (1765: London: Cadell 1809)

Amanda Foreman, 'A politician's politician: Georgiana, Duchess of Devonshire and the Whig party', in Barker and Chalus (eds.), *Gender in Eighteenth Century England* p. 197

E.M. Forster, *Aspects of the Novel* (New York: Harcourt 1927)

Michel Foucault, *Discipline and Punish: The Birth of the Prison* (transl. Alan Sheridan, London: Allen Lane 1977)

T.P. Gallanis, 'The Rise of Modern Evidence Law' 84 *Iowa Law Review* (1999) 499

V.A.C. Gatrell, *The Hanging Tree: Execution and the English People* (Oxford University Press 1994)

Vic Gatrell, *City of Laughter* (London: Atlantic Books 2006)

Johanna Geyer-Kordesch, 'Infanticide and the erotic plot: a feminist reading of eighteenth century crime' in Mark Jackson (ed.), *Infanticide: historical perspectives on child murder and concealment, 1550–2000* pp. 93–127

Hal Gladfelder, *Criminality and Narrative in Eighteenth Century England* (London and Baltimore: Johns Hopkins University Press 2001)

David F. Greenberg, 'The Gendering of Crime in Marxist Theory' in Greenberg (ed.), *Crime and Capitalism: Readings in Marxist Criminology* (2nd ed, Temple University Press 1993)

Harriet Guest, *Small Change: Women, Leaning, Patriotism, 1750–1810* (Chicago and London: University of Chicago Press 2000)

Ian Hacking, *Rewriting the Soul: Multiple Personality and the Sciences of Memory* (Princeton University Press 1995)

Ruth Harris, *Murders and Madness: Medicine, Law and Society in the Fin de Siècle* (Oxford University Press 1989)

Douglas Hay, 'Property, Authority and Criminal Law' in D. Hay, P. Linebaugh and E.P. Thompson (eds.), *Albion's Fatal Tree* (Harmondsworth: Penguin 1975) pp. 17–63

Frances Heidensohn, *Women and Crime* (New York University Press 1985)

Frances Heidensohn and Loraine Gelsthorpe, 'Gender and Crime' in Mike Maguire, Rod Morgan and Robert Reiner (eds.), *The Oxford Handbook of Criminology* (4th ed, Oxford University Press 2007) p. 381

Boyd Hilton, *A Mad, Bad, and Dangerous People? England 1783–1846* (The New Oxford History of England: Oxford University Press 2006)

Jeremy Horder, *Provocation and Responsibility* (Oxford: Clarendon Press 1992)

Jeremy Horder, 'Two Histories and Four Hidden Principles of *Mens Rea*' 113 *Law Quarterly Review* (1997) 95

David Hume, *Enquiry Concerning Human Understanding* (1748: Oxford University Press 1999)

David Hume, *A Treatise of Human Nature* (1739–40: Oxford University Press 2000)

E.J. Hundert, 'The European Enlightenment and the History of the Self', in Roy Porter (ed.), *Rewriting the Self* p. 72

Lynn Hunt, *Inventing Human Rights: A History* (New York: W.W. Norton 2007)

J. Paul Hunter, *Before Novels: the Cultural Contexts of Eighteenth-Century English Fiction* (New York: Norton 1990)

Luce Irigaray, *Thinking the Difference* (London: Athlone Press 1994)

Mary Jacobus, 'Tess's Purity' 26 *Essays in Criticism* (1976) 318–38, reprinted as 'Tess: The Making of a Pure Woman' in Susan Lipshitz (ed.), *Tearing the Veil: Essays on Femininity* (London: Routledge and Kegan Paul 1978) pp. 77–92

Mark Jackson (ed.), *Infanticide: Historical Perspectives on Child Murder and Concealment, 1550–2000* (Ashgate: Aldershot 2002)

Samuel Johnson, 'The fiction of the present age', *The Rambler* (31 March 1750)

Gareth Stedman Jones, *Outcast London: A Study in the Relationship Between Classes in Victorian Society* (Oxford: Clarendon Press 1971; 2nd ed, Penguin 1984)

Elizabeth P. Judge, *Character Witnesses: Credibility and Testimony in the Eighteenth Century Novel* (D.Phil. thesis, Dalhousie University 2004)

Jenny Kermode and Garthine Walker (eds.), *Women, Crime and the Courts in Early Modern England* (London: UCL Press 1994)

Thomas Keymer and Peter Sabor, *Pamela in the Marketplace: Literary Controversy and Print Culture in Eighteenth Century Britain and Ireland* (Cambridge University Press 2005)

Peter King, *Crime, Justice and Discretion 1740–1820* (Oxford University Press 2000)

Peter King, *Crime and Law in England 1750–1840* (Past and Present Publications: Cambridge University Press 2006)

Nicola Lacey, 'In Search of the Responsible Subject: History, Philosophy and Criminal Law Theory' 64 *Modern Law Review* (2001) 350–71

Nicola Lacey, 'Responsibility and Modernity in Criminal Law' 9 *Journal of Political Philosophy* (2001) 249–77

Nicola Lacey, 'Character, Capacity, Outcome: Towards a framework for assessing the shifting pattern of criminal responsibility in modern English law' in Markus Dubber and Lindsay Farmer (eds.), *Modern Histories of Crime and Punishment* (Stanford University Press 2007) pp. 14–41

Norma Landau, *The Justices of the Peace 1679–1760* (Berkeley and Los Angeles: University of California Press 1984)

Norma Landau (ed.), *Law Crime and English Society 1660–1830* (Cambridge University Press 2002)

Stephan Landsman, 'The Rise of the Contentious Spirit: Adversary Procedure in Eighteenth Century England' 75 *Cornell Law Review* (1990) 497–609

John H. Langbein, 'The Criminal Trial before the Lawyers' 45 *University of Chicago Law Review* (1978) 263–316

John H. Langbein, 'Shaping the Eighteenth Century Criminal Trial: A View from the Ryder Sources' 50 *University of Chicago Law Review* (1983) 1–136

John H. Langbein, *The Origins of Adversary Criminal Trial* (Oxford University Press 2003)

Bruce Lenman and Geoffrey Parker, 'The State, the Community and Criminal Law in Early Modern Europe' in V.A.C. Gatrell, Bruce Lenman and Geoffrey Parker (eds.), *Crime and the Law* (London: Europa 1980) p. 11

Gerald Leonard, 'Towards a Legal History of American Criminal Theory: Culture and Doctrine from Blackstone to the Model Penal Code' 6 *Buffalo Criminal Law Review* (2003) 691–832

Jane Lewis, *Women in England 1870–1950* (Bloomington: Indiana University Press 1984)

John Locke *An Essay Concerning Human Understanding* (1690: Oxford University Press 1979)

John E. Loftis, 'Trials and the Shaping of Identity in Tom Jones' 34
   Studies in the Novel (2002) 1
Arlie Loughnan, 'Manifest Madness: Towards a New Understanding of the
   Insanity Defence' 70 *Modern Law Review* (2007) 379–401
Arlie Loughnan, *Mental Incapacity Defences in Criminal Law* (Ph.D. thesis,
   London School of Economics, 2008)
Deidre Shauna Lynch, *The Economy of Character: Novels, Market Culture and the
   Business of Inner Meaning* (University of Chicago Press 1998)
Alan MacFarlane, *The Origins of English Individualism: The Family, Property and
   Social Transition* (Cambridge University Press 1979)
Thomas Mackenzie, 'On Novel-Writing' XX *The Lounger* (18 June 1785)
Josephine McDonagh, *Child Murder and British Culture 1720–1900* (Cambridge
   University Press 2003)
Victoria McGeer, 'Moral travel and the narrative work of forgiveness', paper
   on file with the author
Michael McKeon, *The Origins of the English Novel 1600–1740* (Baltimore: Johns
   Hopkins University Press 1987)
Bernard Mandeville, *The Fable of the Bees or, Private Vices, Publick Benefits* (1723)
   in E.J. Hundert (ed.), *The Fable of the Bees and Other Writings* (Indianapolis:
   Hackett 1997)
John Martin, *Beyond Belief: The Real Life of Daniel Defoe* (Ebbw Vale: Accent
   Press 2006)
Allyson M. May, *The Bar and the Old Bailey 1750–1850* (Chapel Hill: University
   of North Carolina Press 2003)
Juliet Mitchell, 'Moll Flanders, The Rise of Capitalist Woman' pp. 195–218 of
   Women: The Longest Revolution (London: Virago 1984); reprinted from her
   introduction to *Moll Flanders* (Harmondsworth: Penguin 1978)
Franco Moretti, *The Way of the World: The Bildungsroman in European Culture*
   (transl. Albert Sbragia, London: Verso 2000)
Gwenda Morgan and Peter Rushton, *Rogues, Thieves and the Rule of Law: the
   problem of law enforcement in north-east England, 1718–1800* (London: UCL
   Press 1998)
Allison Morris, *Women, Crime and Criminal Justice* (Oxford: Basil Blackwell
   1987)
John Mullan, 'Novels and Feelings' in Roy Porter (ed.), *Rewriting the Self*
   p. 119
Ngaire Naffine, *Female Crime: the Construction of Women in Criminology* (Sydney:
   Allen and Unwin 1987)
Ruth Perry, 'Colonising the Breast: Sexuality and Maternity' *Journal of the
   History of Sexuality* (1991) 204–34
Ruth Perry, *Novel Relations: The Transformations of Kinship in English Literature
   and Culture 1748–1818* (Cambridge University Press 2004)
Coleman Phillipson, *Three Criminal Law Reformers: Beccaria, Bentham, Romilly,*
   (London and Toronto: J.K. Dent and Sons, 1923)

Luke Owen Pike, *A History of Crime in England* Vols 1 and 2 (London: Smith, Elder and Co., 1873–1876)

Otto Pollack, *The Criminality of Women* (Philadelphia: University of Pennsylvania Press 1950)

Roy Porter (ed.), *Rewriting the Self: Histories from the Renaissance to the Present* (London and New York: Routledge 1997)

Richard A. Posner, *Law and Literature: A Misunderstood Relation* (Cambridge: Harvard University Press 1988)

David Punter, 'Fictional Representation of Law in the 18th Century' 16 *Eighteenth-Century Studies* (1982) 47–74

Dana Y. Rabin, *Identity, Crime, and Legal Responsibility in Eighteenth-Century England* (New York: Palgrave Macmillan 2004)

Lisa Rodensky, *The Crime in Mind: Criminal Responsibility and the Victorian Novel* (Oxford University Press 2003)

Richard Rorty, *Philosophy and the Mirror of Nature* (Princeton University Press 1979)

Nikolas Rose, *Governing the Soul: The Shaping of the Private Self* (1989: 2nd ed, London and New York: Free Association Books 1999)

Jan-Melissa Schramm, *Testimony and Advocacy in Victorian Law, Literature and Theology* (Cambridge University Press 2000)

Richard Sennett, *The Fall of Public Man* (London: Faber 1977)

Steven Shapin, *A Social History of Truth: Civility and Science in Seventeenth-Century England* (University of Chicago Press 1983)

Barbara Shapiro, *Probability and Certainty in Seventeenth-Century England: A Study of the Relationships between Natural Science, Religion, History, Law and Literature* (Princeton University Press 1983)

Barbara Shapiro, 'Religion and the Law: evidence, proof and "matter of fact", 1660–1700', in Norma Landau (ed.), *Law Crime and English Society 1660–1830* p. 185

Jim Sharpe, 'Women, Witchcraft and the Legal Process', in Kermode and Walker (eds.), *Women, Crime and the Courts in Early Modern England* pp. 106–24

Robert Shoemaker, *Gender in English Society 1660–1850: The Emergence of Separate Spheres?* (London: Longman 1998)

Susan Skedd, 'Women teachers and the expansion of girls' schooling in England, c. 1760–1820' in Barker and Chalus (eds.), *Gender in Eighteenth Century England*, p. 101

Carol Smart, *Women, Crime and Criminology* (London: Sage 1976)

Adam Smith, *The Theory of Moral Sentiments* (1759: New York: Cosimo 2007)

Bruce Smith: 'The Presumption of Guilt in the English Law of Theft 1750–1850' 23 *Law and History Review* (2005) 133

K.J.M. Smith, *Lawyers, Legislators and Theorists* (Oxford University Press 1998)

Roger Smith, *Trial by Medicine: Insanity and Responsibility in Victorian Trials* (Edinburgh University Press 1981)

Patricia Meyer Spacks, *Imagining a Self: Autobiography and Novel in Eighteenth Century England* (Cambridge: Harvard University Press 1976)

George A. Starr, *Defoe and Casuistry* (Princeton University Press 1971)

Sir James Fitzjames Stephen, *The Story of Nuncomar and the Impeachment of Sir Elijah Impey* (1885: Cornell Library Digital Collections, http://www.library.cornell.edu)

Lawrence Stone, *The Family, Sex and Marriage in England, 1500–1800* (London: Weidenfeld and Nicolson 1977)

Lawrence Stone, *Broken Lives: Separation and Divorce in England 1660–1857* (Oxford University Press 1993)

Naomi Tadmor, *Family and Friends in Eighteenth-Century England: Household, Kinship, and Patronage* (Cambridge University Press 2001)

Charles Taylor, *Sources of the Self: The Making of Modern Identity* (Cambridge University Press 1989)

Charles Taylor, *Modern Social Imaginaries* (Durham: Duke University Press 2004)

E.P. Thompson, *Whigs and Hunters* (Harmondsworth: Penguin 1975)

Janet Todd, *Sensibility: An Introduction* (London: Methuen 1987)

Claire Tomalin, *Jane Austen: A Life* (rev. ed, Harmondsworth: Penguin 2000)

Sylvana Tomaselli, 'The Death and Rebirth of Character in the 18th Century' in Roy Porter (ed.), *Rewriting the Self* p. 84

Lionel Trilling, *Sincerity and Authenticity* (Cambridge: Harvard University Press 1972)

Randolph Trumbach, *The Rise of the Egalitarian Family: Aristocratic Kinship and Domestic Relations in Eighteenth-Century England* (New York: Academic Press 1978)

Mariana Valverde, *Diseases of the Will: Alcohol and the Dilemmas of Freedom* (Cambridge University Press 1998)

Amanda Vickery, 'Golden Age to Separate Spheres? A Review of the Categories and Chonology of English Women's History' 36 *The Historical Journal* (1993) 412

Dror Wahrman, *Imagining the Middle Class* (Cambridge University Press 1995)

Dror Wahrman, *The Making of the Modern Self* (New Haven: Yale University Press 2004)

Garthine Walker, 'Women, Theft and the World of Stolen Goods' in Kermode and Walker (eds.), *Women, Crime and the Courts in Early Modern England* pp. 81–105

Garthine Walker, *Crime, Gender and Social Order in Early Modern England* (Cambridge University Press 2003)

Judith R. Walkowitz, *Prostitution and Victorian Society: Women, Class and the State* (Cambridge University Press 1980)

Ian Ward, *Law and Literature: Possibilities and Perspectives* (Cambridge University Press 1995)

Ian Watt, *The Rise of the Novel: Studies in Defoe, Richardson and Fielding* (Berkeley: University of California Press; London: Chatto and Windus 1957; Hogarth Press 1987)

James Boyd White, *Acts of Hope: Creating Authority in Literature, Law and Politics* (University of Chicago Press 1995)

Martin Wiener, *Reconstructing the Criminal: Culture, Law and Policy in England, 1830–1914* (Cambridge University Press 1991)

Martin Wiener, *Men of Blood: Violence, Manliness and Criminal Justice in Victorian England* (Cambridge University Press 2004)

Carolyn A. Williams, 'Another Self in the Case: Gender, Marriage and the Individual in Augustan Literature' in Roy Porter (ed.), *Rewriting the Self* p. 97

Richard H. Weisberg and Jean-Pierre Barricelli, 'Literature and the Law' in Joseph Gibaldi and Jean-Pierre Barricelli (eds.), *Interrelations of Literature* (New York: MLA 1982)

Alexander Welsh, *Strong Representations: Narrative and Circumstantial Evidence in England* (Baltimore and London: Johns Hopkins University Press 1992)

Arlene Fish Wilner, 'Henry Fielding and the Knowledge of Character' 18(1) *Modern Language Studies* (1988) 181–94

Mary Wollstonecraft, *A Vindication of the Rights of Woman* (1792: Penguin Classics 1985)

Alex Woloch, *The One vs. the Many: Minor Characters and the Space of the Protagonist in the Novel* (Princeton University Press 2003)

Virginia Woolf, 'Defoe' in *The Common Reader* (1925: New York: Harvest, Harcourt 1984) pp. 86–94

Lucia Zedner, *Women, Crime and Custody in Victorian England* (Oxford University Press 1991)

John P. Zomchick, *Family and Law in Eighteenth Century Fiction* (Cambridge University Press 1993)

Index